The Manager's Pocket Guide to Engaging the Aging Workforce

Peter R. Garber
and
Joseph Mack, III

HRD Press v Amherst, MA

Published by: HRD Press, Inc.
                 22 Amherst Road
                 Amherst, Massachusetts 01002
                 1-800-822-2801 (U.S. and Canada)
                 (413) 253-3488
                 (413) 253-3490 (fax)
                 http://www.hrdpress.com

ISBN 978-1-61014-409-4

Production services by Jean Miller
Cover design by Eileen Klockars
Editorial services by Sally Farnham

The Manager's Pocket Guide to Engaging the Aging Workforce

Table of Contents

Preface

*"I will not make age an issue in this campaign.
I'm not going to exploit for political purposes
my opponent's youth and inexperience."*

Quote by President Ronald Reagan concerning his political opponent's age during the second presidential debate with Democratic nominee Walter Mondale in 1984. Reagan was 73 at the time, Mondale was 56.

The point Ronald Reagan so adeptly hammered home is that age is largely a matter of perspective. From his perspective, his age could be viewed as an asset, not a liability. Reagan was able to diffuse the growing campaign issue of his age by this now famous response, which simultaneously made and proved the point that he shouldn't be counted out simply because of his age. The electorate agreed. It hired Reagan for another four years despite his age and he went on to cement his place in history as one of the most respected and influential world leaders of recent times.

As Baby Boomers reach traditional retirement age, the issue of age will become increasingly prominent in our society, including in the workplace. Better health, higher life expectancy, financial concerns, and the desire to continue to be active and productive impel workers to keep working longer. This places them increasingly in direct competition with younger workers for available jobs.

And workers are not just working longer because they need or want a job—employers need them too. The loss of the skills and experience of older workers who are able and ready to retire poses a challenge for many employers in an era of lean staffing where there often are no second stringers on the bench ready to take the places of retiring workers. So too, as a matter of sheer demographics, there may not be enough workers to replace all of the Boomers as they leave the workforce.

Thus, employers are faced with the reality of an aging workforce and the growing dilemma of how to take the fullest advantage of their older workers.

Unfortunately, however, the subject of the older worker is one that many company managers find difficult to discuss openly. Unquestionably, any suggestion that age and performance are somehow linked is fraught with peril in our litigious society. No intelligent manager would wish to be on record as even considering such a possibility, especially if the manager might ever be called upon to make difficult personnel decisions that impact older workers.

Perhaps it is time for a frank dialogue on this subject, however. Is there any truth in the notion that performance on the job usually declines with age?

The authors believe that, except in certain occupations (e.g., professional athlete), there is no inherent link between performance and age. On the other hand, it is obvious that in many instances the overall effort and performance level of the longer service employee often does not match either his or her previous level or that of his or her younger peers. Many reasons can be cited for this phenomenon. We believe that the main reason is loss of engagement—the loss of the desire to perform at the highest level possible each and every day.

Loss of engagement stems from many causes, but not from age. One is the normal career cycle of the average worker. Even those of us who have been outstanding performers throughout our careers will at some point reach our apex position at which our skills and abilities have been maxed out, and from which we are not going to progress any further. No matter how talented and energetic we believe we still are, we will start to realize that our career now "is what it is" and what it is going to be. When workers start getting the internal and external inklings that they have reached this point, they may react in a variety of ways. Some will choose to at least attempt to move on and find a better opportunity elsewhere. But for most, that is not a reality. They may react with resignation, apathy, depression, or even anger. It is amazing and sad how many long service workers who have had rewarding careers with a company end up leaving their jobs, whether voluntarily or involuntarily, in a state of anger and disenchantment.

Loss of engagement can also be caused by signals sent to older workers by an employer telling them that they are no longer viewed as valued members of the team or as part of the team's future. These signals can take several forms: unexplained lowering of performance ratings when performance seems to have remained constant; lack of inclusion in new projects or meetings; stagnation or lowering in raises and bonuses for no obvious reason; etc. These signals usually are not being sent intentionally or maliciously. Most often, they are the result of managers being faced with the task of doling out limited financial resources and job opportunities in a way that ensures the future health of the company. Not everyone can advance continuously when it comes to raises, bonuses, and promotions. Managers must decide whether it is better to reward the steady, good performance of their long-term workers who are unlikely to exit the company even if disappointed, or to reward the workers who are viewed as the future of the company and far more likely to bolt over failure to recognize them.

For these and other reasons, some older workers may lose the level of engagement they once had. Their performance level stagnates or even decreases. They may become cynical about the company and its leaders. They may decide to coast to retirement or until the tap on the shoulder telling them it is time to leave. All in all, they are in a place that benefits neither them nor their employers.

We believe this scenario is not inevitable. Good leaders—leaders who are both engaged and engaging—can and should make an effort to keep the engagement levels of senior workers high and thereby capitalize on and leverage talents of such workers rather than permit them to wither, become morale killers, and hold back the company from meeting its goals. We hope this book gets you thinking about how you might become such a leader.

Introduction

Career Lifeboat

Here's a story: Seven executives go out on a sailboat one afternoon for some deep-sea fishing, and to enjoy the ocean breeze, talk about business a bit, and just relax. Suddenly, an unexpected storm hits, and the boat is rocked back and forth as the waves bounce it around as if it were a cork in a bathtub. All hands are immediately on deck as they struggle to save the boat and more importantly their lives. All of their navigational and communications equipment, including their cell phones, is damaged by the ocean waves pounding relentlessly into the boat. It becomes apparent that they have to abandon ship, but they are shocked to find out that the lifeboat on board will hold only six people. It is certain that overloading this lifeboat with even one extra person will seriously threaten the safety of everyone if they should choose that course of action given the rough waters and storm's growing intensity. They are confronted with a terrible decision—who should be given a seat on this lifeboat and who should remain behind to face almost certain doom? On board is the company CEO, chief financial officer, IT director, marketing director, public relations manager, operations director, and human resource director. A debate ensues concerning the relative value of each of these seasoned and highly experienced individuals in dealing with this serious dilemma in which they find themselves and even more difficult: the decision of who will be left behind.

There was immediate consensus that the CEO should be given a seat, despite his insistence he stay behind citing the fact that he is the oldest in the group and has already lived a long and full life, as everyone recognized the need for strong leadership on this challenge they are about to face. The chief financial officer argues that they will need his years of expertise in budgeting and allocating the limited supplies and resources that they will have on this tiny lifeboat. The IT director claims that his experience in technical matters may be able to get at least one of their cell phones working given enough time, which they apparently will have plenty of as they drift aimlessly at sea. The marketing director, always thinking about business, presents his ideas about how the company could use this experience to more effectively market the company's products and services, something the CEO in particular sees as of potential value. The operations director claims that his years of knowledge and expertise in making things work effectively and efficiently will be critical to their survival at sea. The public relations manager makes the case for himself by pointing out just how important media and investor relations will be when they get back from this ordeal at sea. He makes a persuasive argument about the advantage of having an experienced spokesperson's first-hand account of this adventure, noting that this story will get national media coverage and be great free publicity for the organization, perhaps making the company a more attractive investment as the others think about their currently deflating incentive bonus plans funded with company stock. Then it dawns on everyone that the HR director's pitch for a seat on the lifeboat has not been heard. He argues that there are certain to be disputes during such a dangerous and stressful ordeal that they are about to undertake and they will need his years of expertise in sensitive negotiations and conflict resolution to keep everyone working productively together as a team during this real-life crisis they are about to experience.

The group quickly contemplates the rationale and arguments presented by each leader. Time is running out as their boat is starting to sink into the sea and the decision of who will remain behind must be made quickly or they all will perish. Which of the seven leaders do you think would be selected for the six seats on the lifeboat? In the end, each of these individual's arguments for a seat on the lifeboat will ultimately be judged by the perception of the others about the value of each person's knowledge, experience, and expertise gained over their lifetimes and careers to help them survive this crisis.

In actuality, we all play this survival exercise virtually every day at work. Our career survival is ultimately determined by the value (or, just as importantly, the perceived value) we create for the organization as we perform our jobs. But what role does experience play in this equation? How valuable do you think the experience that employees gain over their careers is to the survival of the organization?

Continuing with the survival theme, some organizations find themselves struggling both in good times and bad, seemingly adrift at sea without direction. Either they cannot handle success or do not know how to deal with the problems they face during difficult times. Even success can be a daunting challenge. You have to be able to deal with success and the challenges and changes it can bring such as increased manpower needs, demand for more sophisticated processes, or sustainability of past performance levels. On the other end of the spectrum, problems organizations face must be prevented from becoming crises. Experienced leaders can play an important role in helping organizations not only deal with these challenges but to help build processes to prevent reentering these shark-infested waters again in the future. Experience should caution organizations to make sure that there are always enough seats for everyone on the lifeboat just in case there are rough waters looming over the horizon. In the final analysis, your older, more experienced workers will likely be the first to remind you of this sage advice.

This book is about the value that older workers bring to the organizations that employ them. You might think that this should be an obvious and seemingly easy argument to make. Unfortunately, this is not the mindset that many organizations may have concerning this segment of their employee population. This book will examine many of our current beliefs, practices, and misconceptions about older workers, particularly with the changes resulting from the expanding lifespans and more active lifestyles of the older segment of our population and their impact on the workplace of tomorrow. At the conclusion of each chapter are included discussion points concerning the material covered to stimulate dialogue and hopefully actions relating to these important potential issues concerning the older workers in your organization.

Chapter 1

Learning to Engage Older Workers

We believe that a good place to begin our discussion of engaging older workers is with the subject of engagement itself, and how to become an engaged and engaging leader. We hear much about the benefits of employee engagement today, but the concept of engagement can be very confusing. The problem is that employee engagement can mean many different things in our organizations today. Employee engagement is one of those business ideals that most companies desire but do not know exactly how to accomplish. When you begin to talk about engaging the older segment of your employee population, this concept gets even *grayer.* (Pun intended!)

Although based on relatively simple concepts, it can be very challenging to successfully introduce an employee-engagement initiative in an organization. Every function of the organization plays an important role in helping the organization create and sustain an engaged workforce. It requires the support and dedication of your entire organization, particularly that of top management. Many employee engagement initiatives fail to reach their goals and objectives because of a lack of leadership's committed involvement in the process. For leaders, engagement is actually a two-way street. Employee engagement starts with leaders who are not just fully engaged in their job but who also practice the art of engaging leadership. Without leadership that is both engaged and engaging, it will be very difficult—if not impossible—to engage the rest of the organization.

To be engaging, leaders first need to be fully engaged in the operation of the business going beyond their traditional roles. If they are not engaged themselves, leaders will not be engaging—they will not make others desire to be engaged, and, consequently, they will not be able to have maximum impact in helping the organization reach its goals for success.

To engage employees, leadership must begin by demonstrating its own engagement and its commitment to creating a culture of engagement. This means taking a dynamic, progressive, and optimistic role in leading the organization in the direction in which it needs to go to survive in the competitive business world today. An engaging leader drives employee engagement throughout the organization on all levels to help everyone—including those older, more experienced employees who are often overlooked in these initiatives—reach their greatest potential.

One thing that you will find is that when it comes to becoming an engaging leader, one size does not fit all. While studies have suggested that engaging leaders share certain common traits, they do not necessarily act the same. You need to find your own style of an "engaging leader hat" to wear: one that feels and hopefully looks best on you. You must become comfortable in your leadership style when it comes to engaging employees. Regardless of your level of expertise, experience, or the amount of time that you have spent working as a leader, you need to have resources available that can help answer many of the complex problems and questions you will face every day. You will not be expected to know all the answers, but you need to know where to go for advice and direction when needed.

Engaging leadership plays a unique role in today's organizations. Leaders, by their very nature, must look at things differently than the rest of the organization. While everyone else is working toward fulfilling the mission or purpose in the organization, engaging leaders need to be focused not simply on that goal but also on how the organization functions and countless issues that are related to ensuring that the needs of the organization are met not only today but in the future.

Here is where the complexity of becoming an engaging leader begins. To be truly engaging, a leader must not only fully understand the strategy and direction of the organization, but also help others understand these objectives and be fully committed to realizing the organization's overall mission. In short, today's leader must lead the workforce to become fully engaged. Leading the organization toward employee engagement can be an important factor in helping reach the goals and objectives of the organization in the future. This is an opportunity for engaging leaders to really add value to the organization by leveraging all of its resources, including older workers.

Communicating as a Leader

There is a communications technique that every attorney who has presented a case in court seems to know. When interrogating a witness at trial, the unwritten rule is that you should never ask a question to which you do not already know the answer. An attorney does not want to be surprised by new evidence or information that might ruin his or her case. By knowing the answer in advance, the attorney avoids unpleasant, case-destroying surprises. She maintains control of her case and the ability to ask follow-up questions in a manner that elicits the evidence that best supports her client's desired ruling or remedy from the court. The point is that we need to communicate with a well-thought-out purpose or even a strategy in mind. You should have a goal in every communication that you engage in with another person. Your communication goal may be as simple as just to stay in touch and see how the other person is doing. This is a perfectly good objective as it helps to build and maintain working relationships. Or your goal might be to discuss something of great importance and consequence. In either case, you have a goal or an objective in mind that you are expecting to achieve in your communication.

So much of our success as leaders is about being able to communicate effectively with others and with purpose. In most situations in life, you will not know the answers to everything that you would ask others in your personal interactions like the lawyer in court. But you should ask questions that show that you are interested in the other person and what he or she has to say. People's favorite subject is typically themselves. If you want to develop greater rapport with people, ask them about their goals rather than try to tell them about yours. An engaging leader is a good listener.

This is especially true when communicating to older employees about their hopes and goals for their future careers. Listen for what is truly important to them concerning this part of their lives. You need to remain aware of the fact that the financial situation they may find themselves in today is one that they never expected and may have significantly changed their future plans including when they expected and wanted to retire. This is probably a significant change in their lives, and they may want to express their feelings and concerns about this life-changing turn of events with you, so you need to be prepared to have this discussion. You need to listen with empathy to their needs and work together to find ways to accommodate their desire to continue working and reaching their ultimate retirement goals.

Becoming more effective in your communications can help you better achieve whatever goals you hope to reach as a leader. To become a better communicator, you may need to think about communications a bit differently than you do now. You should think about your communications with others as an opportunity to learn more about the people who work for you. Again, asking questions about them is obviously one way to learn more about people and their lives. But there is so much more that you can possibly learn about others as a result of your communications with them. Gaining a better understanding about how someone might feel about a particular issue can be very useful and helpful to you particularly if you need that person to help you reach an important goal in your role as a leader. This is especially true if you are asking older workers about how they feel about their role and future in the organization. You might just be surprised by what they have to tell you in regards to their long-term career goals and aspirations in today's work environment.

And remember, effective communication reaps benefits way beyond just transmitting or eliciting information. The very act of asking a person to share their concerns or ideas and then really listening to his or her response itself encourages engagement in that employee.

The Engaging Leader Perspective

Understanding the proper perspective of an engaging leader is important to anyone who steps into a leadership role. Engaging leaders pay attention to not only the operations of organization but also the human side of running an organization or business. This perspective is sometimes overlooked or even viewed as unimportant by everyone else in the midst of all the other things that must be done in order for the organization to operate. This is where the leader's perspective becomes crucial. Engaging leaders accept the responsibility to ensure that the rest of the organization remains aware of the employee issues that must be properly managed in order to have a successful operation.

It is the job of an engaging leader to keep these issues in the forefront. If these issues are ignored or not given the attention they deserve, they can become costly and even embarrassing problems for the entire organization.

The "Soft Stuff" Is Often the Hardest

Engaging leadership is all about paying attention to the "soft stuff" in managing an organization. The term *soft stuff* refers to the intangible components of any business's success, primarily involving its people rather than its technical operations. The soft stuff can be the hardest to manage. And managing it is just as critical to the organization's success as managing the more tangible things. In fact, it is the soft stuff that causes many of the problems that exist in organizations every day. Millions of dollars may be spent on the technical aspects of an operation or venture only to have it all be negated by some soft-stuff issue not adequately addressed or accounted for in the planning or allocation of resources. Ultimately no matter what size the organization, the way the soft stuff is handled impacts employee engagement. If you do not give the soft stuff your attention proactively, it will get your attention in some other way, usually in the form of a crisis as was the case in the following story.

The Case of the Untrained Experienced Operators

A medium-sized plastics manufacturer had just invested millions of dollars in installing new automated equipment in their Midwest manufacturing facility, which was expected to make the operation much more efficient and ultimately more profitable. The installation process had been painstakingly planned by the engineering group at the divisional headquarters of the company with every conceivable detail addressed to ensure the success of the new process. This became the number-one priority in the company at the moment, and practically every resource available was dedicated to this installation and for good reason as there was a great deal riding on its success. The company had been experiencing significant losses in business during the past few years to their major competitor that had already automated their processes and was able to produce products less expensively and faster. The CEO anxiously waited for the return of this very significant investment and to finally hear some good financial news from the manufacturing operations of the company.

Unfortunately, even after months had passed following the installation and a few start-up "bugs" in the process had been worked out, the production numbers were not meeting expectations. The facility manager was constantly on the phone with divisional headquarters, trying to explain what was wrong. After engineering review after review, it was determined that the equipment was operating exactly as it was designed to, actually at a higher efficiency rating than anticipated. Everyone was wondering why, then, wasn't the process meeting the overall performance levels as expected. Something needed to be done to correct this situation and quickly, as the CEO's patience was wearing very thin. He wanted answers and wanted them now.

The plant manager of the manufacturing facility called yet another emergency meeting of all his direct reports to conduct what he called a "post mortem review" of the installation process and failures. This could well have become a prophetic moniker for the process as not only his career but those of everyone in the room seemed to be in the balance. He went around the room asking once again for a detailed review of all the steps that were taken to ensure the installation process was completed correctly. All the technical departments once again presented the most current detailed graphs, flows charts, schematics, testing results, and other data to demonstrate that everything was installed correctly. Finally, it was the production manager's turn to discuss the people side of the process. He described how the process had created new jobs that had been assigned to employees according to the company's policies, which were primarily based on seniority: those with the most company service, obtaining the highest paying jobs, and so forth down the line.

The plant manager finally thought to ask what training those being assigned to these new jobs had received, recognizing that the new process required many different skills than the old antiquated process. He remembered asking that the production workers have input into not only the installation of the new equipment but also in developing the training programs for operating this equipment. The plant manager had assumed that these workers had been engaged in all of these aspects of the process and as a result would feel a sense of ownership for their training on this new equipment. To his surprise, the production manager explained that with all the focus on the installation of the new equipment that there admittedly had not been as much attention as he had hoped to be paid on training for these employees in the new jobs. The idea of having these employees engaged in developing these training programs just kept getting pushed aside as the installation always seemed to be the top priority of the day. In addition, the assumption was that as most of these employees had many years of experience, some of them over 25 or 30 or more, that they would just naturally know how to operate the new equipment. These workers had also been involved in much of the actual physical installation of the new equipment, and it was just also assumed that this would make them familiar with what they would need to do to operate this equipment.

Unfortunately, that was not the case as this group was just beginning to realize. During this review, it was determined that almost all of the production problems that they were presently experiencing could be associated with this lack of training of the production workers who were actually operating the process. Although the majority of these employees were very experienced, this knowledge was actually becoming counter-productive. They had been trying to use their skills and experience running the old process on the new equipment, and this simply was just not working. Somehow, no one up until this point had made the connection between this lack of training provided to them with the problems the process was experiencing. It was just presumed because these employees had been with the company for so long performing their jobs that they would just naturally know how to operate this new equipment. As it turned out, this was simply not true.

The plant manager ordered the production process to temporarily stop until these employees could be properly trained on their new jobs. This time, these older workers were given the opportunity to provide their input into the new process, which turned out to be very insightful and innovative. They helped develop an extensive training process for all the workers involved in this new process, resulting in excellent results. They also appreciated being given the opportunity to share their ideas and actually see them implemented. This indeed did give them a sense of ownership of the training programs they developed, and they helped more junior employees become familiar and competent in their new responsibilities. The overall cost of this training would have been much less if conducted before the production process had restarted after the installation of the new equipment but was still minimal compared to the overall investment in this project and what was at stake. Once this training was completed, the process soon began to not only meet but exceed the production goals it had been designed to achieve.

Everyone was amazed how after spending millions of dollars on the installation of the new equipment, something as basic as making sure these experienced senior operators were trained on the new equipment could have been overlooked.

Constant Vigilance Needed

Leaders need to be constantly vigilant to ensure that these kinds of issues are being given the attention they deserve. Otherwise, even the most carefully planned and executed projects can come crashing down because of a soft-stuff issue such as what occurred in this story, especially if you are making erroneous assumptions about your older workforce and their needs to continue to be successful in performing their jobs. Think about how many times you may have made this mistake of assuming that an experienced employee was aware of something new being introduced into the job without providing him or her with the training or resources needed to perform their job properly.

The point is that we need to be careful not to overlook the needs of older experienced workers because of assumptions we might make about their current skills and potential. In this case, the company failed to provide them with the proper training they needed to perform their jobs after new equipment was introduced into their workplace. Perhaps even more common is the perception that older workers are less capable of learning new skills because of their age. To truly engage older workers, you need to make sure that they have all the training and resources necessary to continue to be successful in their jobs and careers. To do otherwise is simply not fair to these older employees and in reality, setting them up for failure.

How Well Do You Manage Change?

The answer to this question will be important to your effort to engage your organization's workers, particularly your highly experienced older workers. Willingness to embrace change is a sign of how engaged a worker really is.

Many leaders presume that older workers will resist change. Is that based in fact or is it a stereotype? Most often the greatest hindrance to successfully introducing change lies not in ingrained attitudes of employees but in poor implementation. Poorly implemented change fosters the "whatever" attitude symptomatic of disengagement.

If you pay little or no attention to how things being changed are affecting people, you are not managing change very effectively, especially when it concerns your older employees. Most workers, and especially long service workers, become suspicious of change that affects them when it is not clear what the reasons and benefits are. Is this change meaningful and long lasting or merely a new "flavor of the month" instituted by new management just to show that it is doing something? Did the decision to make this change take into account the input of and affect upon those closest to the process being changed? Is this change just an excuse for culling employees? Is this new program really novel or just a "been there, done that" situation? Such concerns are not necessarily the product of the older workers' innate feelings of victimization or natural resistance to anything that will cause them to exert more effort. They can be a result of workers' personal experience with poorly implemented or unsuccessful past initiatives. Paradoxically, they can also be grounded in the workers' strong sense of ownership in the company and in their jobs—in their honest desire to see change that brings good results rather than change for the sake of change. Older workers understand that change is both inevitable and necessary for growth. But it is easier to accept change when the people telling you it is necessary have earned your trust.

Communicating about changes as far in advance as possible will give everyone a chance to get used to what is going to be different and be better able to adjust to these changes. Highlighting the positive opportunities created by the changes and how individuals could benefit can help favorably affect their attitudes about the change itself. Being as transparent as you can will also cut down on the speculations and rumors that might be created as a result of the impending change, including the reasons, goals, and expected benefits of these initiatives. Reaching out to those who you know have the most difficulty dealing with change by helping them better understand how they may or may not be affected by the change also is important to help those who tend to resist change the most to adapt more readily.

Most importantly, to be an engaging leader, you have to be passionate about the changes that you are about to introduce. Emotionally accepting change is perhaps the first and most important step in the process of successful implementation. This must begin with you as a leader embracing this change. You cannot just go through the motions of supporting change; you must believe in the changes you are introducing and take the time and effort to help others do the same. You also have to be careful not to fall into the mistaken mindset of assuming that your older workers are less likely to accept or adapt to change than younger employees, as this perception will cause you to send a negative signal to your workers both young and old, and become a self-fulfilling assumption. In fact, older workers by virtue of the many changes they have seen and experienced over their careers are often better equipped to deal with change than those less experienced.

Practice What You Preach

Too often, leaders say they support change but probably prefer that it happen someplace else in the organization. Consciously or subconsciously, many leaders tend to believe that what they are doing "works" and they do not really need to change anything. They are as resistant to engagement initiatives as anyone else, even when the evidence suggests that their employees lack engagement. In their minds, the problem lies in the employees, not in them.

However, this attitude is bound to torpedo employee engagement initiatives in an organization. You need to lead by example. There can't be an "engagement is the other guy's problem" mentality. If you are going to lead employee engagement in the organization, you must practice it as well. You cannot have the opinion that "I'm all for employee engagement as long as it doesn't involve the way I manage or lead others." Employee engagement works best when everyone has a personal stake in the process, including leaders. Sometimes you just need to take an introspective look at your own feelings and accept the changes that you may be telling others that they must accept, including how you engage the older workers in your organization.

Removing Barriers

There can be many potential barriers to employee engagement that are typically easy to find if you look hard enough for them but not always as easy to remove. Seen from a leader's perspective, this can be a limiting "that's not my responsibility" mindset. It is also fairly easy to get caught in the victim mentality of blaming the organization for your problems. Barriers to achieving employee engagement can exist even in a leader's own backyard. The leader believes he cannot perform better because some lacking resource or organizational barrier is preventing this higher level of performance from becoming possible. Without these changes, the leader feels stuck in a rut that he cannot get out of on his own. This is an example of frustrated leadership that finds nothing but excuses for lack of performance. Engaged leadership starts by addressing barriers—such as policies, practices, procedures, and systems that might be inhibiting employee engagement—head on.

The following story describes such a situation:

Engagement-Sapping Policies

Chris Johnson was the operations director for a company in the business of providing services for the telecommunications industry. He had experienced growing frustration at internal and external customer complaints that the company's customer service personnel, most of whom were long-service workers, were often surly and unresponsive. In other words, they were disengaged. He felt that the bureaucratic policies of the company were dampening enthusiasm and causing disengagement among employees. He was upset by continuously hearing that things that could potentially increase employee engagement could not be implemented because of the company's own rules and procedures. In a meeting to discuss how the organization could move toward a more engaged customer service workforce, Chris asked, "Why does it always seem that our own policies are designed to inhibit our attempts to engage our employees more in their jobs?"

"Hey, take it easy Chris, don't shoot the messenger here. I'm just telling you how it is. We have certain policies and practices in this organization that we have to pay attention to and follow. We can't just go and do anything we want, making up the rules as we go along. Our employees won't know what rules they are supposed to follow if we start doing this kind of thing," Sally Armstrong, the customer service manager replied.

"I understand your point, but it seems like every time we try to do something progressive or even different in the way we manage our company, there is some rule that says we can't!" Chris responded. "I understand that we don't want to appear to be making up the rules as we go, but can't we change the rules once in a while to meet the needs of the future? Isn't that what a progressive company, like we like to think we are, is supposed to do? Maybe we have become too bureaucratic as we have grown."

"What is it that you want to see changed so urgently anyways?" Sally asked.

"For one thing, we need to give your customer service representatives more authority to make decisions concerning service complaints that they receive directly from our customers. Many of the customer service representatives have been with the company for 20 years or more. In fact, all of you know Helen Carlson, who has been a customer service rep for us for nearly 40 years now. Helen and the other CSRs know better than we do what it takes to make our customers happy without "giving away the store," so to speak. Right now they have to go through layers of approvals to make even the simplest of service decisions. I'm not saying that they should make new service policies every time they have a customer complaint, but they do need more discretion than they have now. No one knows how to serve our customers better than they do," Chris responded.

"Chris makes a good point," the president of the company, Henry Franklin, interjected. "We have to do things to differentiate ourselves from the competition, and service is the key to gaining customer satisfaction in our business. We also need to allow our more experienced employees to be able to make decisions, especially ones in which they truly are the subject matter expert. If we don't capitalize on their experience and knowledge, we are denying ourselves one of our greatest resources and, in fact, turning them off to the company. Maybe it's just because I am now part of this older generation in the workplace, but I for one am gaining a new appreciation for the talents and potential of our older workforce. And, if our policies and procedures are limiting our moving in the direction of greater engagement of these folks, then we should look at changing these polices.

"But, I also agree with Sally that this needs to be done right and with some serious thought before making any changes. I would like to create a task force to look at what things we should consider changing: those customer service policies and practices that could be barriers to engaging our employees more in their jobs and most importantly in servicing our customers. I would like everyone on my direct staff to be involved on this task force and report your progress back to me on a regular basis, and I would like to see your final recommendations by the end of the quarter. Remember what we are trying to accomplish here: greater employee engagement for all of our employees, but especially our most experienced and longer-service employees. Don't be afraid to get those who will be directly impacted by these potential changes involved in the change process itself. I would especially like to see Helen on this task force to be able to learn from her many years of experience as well."

The *Habitualized* Organization

Like a fishing boat on the ocean, a company navigating through the business environment can experience dramatic environmental change in an instant with little or no warning and suddenly find itself in troubled waters. Creating a system for responding to these changes is perhaps the greatest challenge and predictor of future success for any organization. The most successful organizations understand the important role that their leaders can play in creating such an organizational capability to change. The most important ability an organization needs in today's competitive global business world is to be able to adapt to changing times. This is when engaging leadership can be most important.

However, many organizations tend to operate in the predictable ways with which they feel most comfortable. This could be called residing in organizational *comfort zones.* Everyone feels that he or she is performing adequately as long as they are involved in these organizational processes anticipated and expected by everyone. This is the "habitualized organization" at its best and worst. Everything is great as long as the business remains strong and there appears to be no adverse consequences to continuing this habitual organizational behavior. Some of these behaviors do support success, but others have no real impact or, in reality, may be having a negative impact. The truth is hidden by the sometimes camouflaged view of positive bottom-line performance. Success covers up many inherent organizational weaknesses. This is the equivalent of a ship's captain being lulled by calm waters with plentiful sunshine and abundant fish to catch into ignoring the ship's navigational systems showing that the ship is veering increasingly off course and into a storm.

A perceived connection between established organizational processes and success can arise to the level of superstition within the company, the equivalent of placing your faith in a rabbit's foot in your pocket. Unfortunately making things even worse, in many organizations it is the leadership of a function that blindly maintains and perpetuates the organization's ritual belief in in the status quo—the polar opposite of truly engaging leadership.

Engagement Requires Questioning Organizational Rituals

Ritualized behavior exists in virtually every organization. Areas where it may be found within a company include, for example, succession planning, strategic business planning processes, operational procedures, recruitment initiatives, public relations programs, budget reviews, orientation processes, promotion requirements, and internal communications protocols just to name a few. The list of these processes or procedures that fall into these cyclical organizational processes could be endless.

Not all organizational rituals or habitual processes are unproductive or unnecessary. Many do serve an important function and need to be relied upon. The point is that someone needs to step up and state what is probably obvious to everyone in the organization about the relative value of at least some of the organization's practices that should no longer be continued or need to be changed. Corporate rituals can become sacred cows, and this can be disastrous especially if it is the leader of the organization who thinks these outmoded rituals are still worthwhile for whatever reason or, even worse, is perceived to have such a blind devotion to them that they may not be questioned by anyone without running the risk of incurring the leader's wrath.

Think about the things that happen on a predictable schedule in your organization. Are some of these just habitual organizational rituals in reality adding little or no value to the organization or even counterproductive to your organization's goals? It is important to be able to differentiate between those rituals that add value and those that do not.

In an organization that fosters employee engagement, the questioning of ritualized behavior is not only permitted but encouraged. Engaged leaders make the effort to learn how to make themselves heard within their organizations and then take the lead in such questioning. An engaging leader creates an environment favorable to such questioning by others and remains open to the possibility that the opinions and ideas of subordinates are valuable even when they question the organization's sacred cows.

The following is an example of an organization perpetuating an unproductive ritualistic process:

Top Talent Search

A large corporation established an annual process for identifying and developing top talent within the organization, especially those considered to be high-potential talent. The selection process for inclusion in this group was extremely cumbersome involving multiple nomination and approval levels. Over time, many of the managers involved in the process as well as employees affected by the process began to question the legitimacy of the process that was thought to have become highly politicized with too many selections not based on dispassionate, objective factors but rather based mostly on the CEO's actual or perceived personal preferences. It also seemed that once selected into this prestigious group, many individuals were anointed for life as top talent regardless of whether their future performance lived up to the hype of their promoters. It also appeared that, with a few exceptions, employees' evaluations and chances of being selected for enhance developmental opportunities diminished with increasing age.

The result was a very time-consuming but ineffective process that added little or no real value to the organization, bestowed limited resources on some employees who were bound to disappoint and, even worse, kept many worthy employees from receiving the developmental opportunities and recognition they deserved, including many older employees. This, in turn, caused workers who perceived the system as benefitting only others to become disengaged because they believed that extraordinary effort or results on their part would never be recognized.

This ritualistic talent program was never challenged because it was perceived to be a sacred cow of the CEO who was understandably very interested in developing top talent in the organization. In truth, the vice president of HR had her own

---

nagging suspicions that the process had become ineffectual and demoralizing, especially to high-performing older workers. She became more and more frustrated when nothing was done to evaluate or improve the process, but she bit her tongue because she did not want to be perceived as a naysayer by the leadership team. And so it goes: problems exist in organizations that everyone is frustrated about but no one ever seems to do anything to correct.

This is a situation where engaging leaders—leaders adamantly open to new ideas—could have been extremely important and valuable. Think about how some or even many of these practices may be adversely impacting your older workers. What would happen if you as a leader suggested that some of these habitual activities in your organization were to no longer be continued? Would you be ostracized from the organization? Or would you be listened to with thoughtful consideration given to your suggestion? Obviously, if you are going to take such a risk, you would want the latter to occur and your suggestions be considered and listened to by others. But how can you as a single individual get your voice heard if you are not the top decision maker in the organization? An important part of being engaged as a leader is figuring out how to get your voice heard. You not only need to speak up, but once you have gotten everyone's attention, you need to make a convincing argument. If you are perceived to be an engaged and engaging leader, people both above and below you in the company food chain will be far more likely to listen to you when you challenge rituals of the organization.

In the example above, the HR VP's reticence to speak up was symptomatic of not just an organization that inhibits engagement, but that she herself did not possess the attributes of an engaging leader.

Getting Your Voice Heard

Getting your voice heard is an important part of becoming an engaging leader. It is not enough to just get a seat at the leaders' lunch table; you also need to be a voice that is respected. You cannot just pound your fist on the table or hold your breath until you turn blue to get everyone's attention, at least not for very long. You have to make convincing and valid points, especially if you are going to be advocating the benefits of employee engagement for older employees to the top decision makers in your organization. You need to look at engaging older employees as a business objective and state your rationale and arguments for their greater engagement in those terms. You will be expected to see what others may be missing regarding the impact that employee engagement can achieve and how it can support whatever direction or changes the organization is thinking about initiating. But making the case for action or change is not always easy. Being reminded that most people are all for change as long as it does not directly change them makes this challenge even more difficult. Your influencing skills may be the most important factor in ensuring that your voice is heard concerning engaging older workers. The following are tips for helping ensure that your voice is heard.

10 Ways to Get Your Voice Heard

1. **Don't become the "great dissenter."** We all know people whose first reaction to anyone else's new idea is always to oppose it. Some people are most comfortable playing the role of the "great dissenter." That way they can avoid taking responsibility if a new idea fails and, better yet, they can play the "I told you so" game. Truly engaged and engaging leaders do not do this. Staking out a contrarian position in knee-jerk fashion will not help you gain the trust and confidence that you need to be influential. For example, too quickly announcing, "I'm against that idea" immediately upon hearing a suggestion

by a colleague may commit you to your contrary position, perhaps without adequate reason or rationale. Be careful not to disagree just for the sake of disagreeing. Sometimes this syndrome is a reaction to a particular person whom you philosophically disagree with on just about everything. But you also need to realize that even that individual may occasionally have a good idea, maybe even a great one. Being predictably against new ideas, no matter how often you may be right in your assessments, has the effect of shutting down others from floating new ideas, even good ones. Usually it is better to withhold your opinion and judgment until you have had a chance to think through an idea or proposal. There are also certain things that simply just aren't worth arguing. You can waste a lot of energy as well as political capital in meaningless squabbles whose outcomes have little or no impact on anyone including you. Don't waste everyone's time on fighting for things that don't really matter.

2. **Become an authority.** Don't expect others to listen to you simply because of your title in the organization. To be trusted, you need the expertise to give good advice and guidance on business matters and concerns. This expertise will not come naturally or just from osmosis, but from doing your homework. Leadership requires dynamic thinking and you will need to put some effort into keeping up with the latest trends and changes as well as their impact on your organization. Your knowledge and understanding should not be just confined to matters within your area of expertise. You also need to understand other aspects or related parts of the business to be able to truly understand their full implications. Do your homework and even take a history lesson or two about what has happened in the business in the past to better understand possible trends in the future. The more you speak from a knowledgeable and educated position, the louder your voice will be heard.

3. **Pay attention to how others feel.** People can become very emotional about a particular topic or issue but not always express these emotions from the onset. Making the effort to try to appreciate how the other person feels about the issue at hand can help you really understand how they stand on that particular issue and to gauge their reaction. So often when an important issue is discussed or even debated, what are really being expressed back and forth are more emotions rather than the associated facts. Taking a cue from these emotions in addition to the actual words being spoken can tell you a great deal about how someone really feels about the issue. Once understood, just acknowledging someone's expressed or unexpressed but evident emotions on a particular issue will tell them that you at least understand how they feel. This is important to people.

   For instance, think about a time when you tried to talk to someone who was really upset about something and was trying to express just how angry he or she was about the issue. Would it be productive to try to engage in a debate about the relative merits of his or her position on the subject at this time? The answer is no. The facts are secondary to the emotions that the person is feeling at that moment. A simple acknowledgment such as, "I can tell that you feel very strongly about this issue," acknowledges that you at least understand how the person is feeling. Following up with another empathetic statement such as, "Help me understand why this issue is so important to you," will lead to much better dialogue and true understanding about why this person is taking a particular adversarial position. It will also make the other person more receptive to what you have to say. With this approach you will be in a much better position to effectively convey your own thoughts about the matter and make your point in a more convincing manner.

   Do not expect or demand that someone who is emotionally overwrought agree with you there and then. This usually only causes them to dig their heels in deeper.

Give them time to re-process what you have said later, on their own. Often they will come around to your ideas on their own after calmer reflection.

4. **Check your facts first, then articulate your rationale.** In order to make a convincing argument, you need to know your facts and articulate them in a logical and understandable manner. Doing your homework is essential. Check your facts and be prepared for them to be challenged. Presenting unsubstantiated information will sink your argument faster than anything. Think about how the most likely critics will present their rebuttal or counterarguments and be prepared to respond.

    Make an outline for yourself giving thought to the best way to present your argument or rationale. You might begin with a brief history of the issue and what worked or didn't work well in the past and why. Be prepared to be interrupted by impatient critics and respond by asking them to hear you out at least for the moment. But remember that attention spans are very limited in meetings. People's patience will be short for listening to too much information, so get to the point. You need to choose your words sparingly and wisely. End with your best argument or strongest point summarizing your rationale. The clearer and more organized your argument, the more likely others will listen to you.

5. **Understand the importance of timing.** Timing is important in most things in the business world. Having the right product at the right time focused on the right customers is what every business seeks to achieve and often determines their success. The same could be said about getting your voice heard by the right people in your organization. You have to be talking about the right thing at the right time and have the right information targeted to the right audience. Timing seems to be one of those things that may be difficult to teach. Some people seem to have an innate sense for when the right time is to do or

say something. It is perhaps easier to describe when the right time *isn't*. For example, if there is some *other* pressing business crisis looming in front of key decision makers, bringing up employee engagement for older workers at that moment may not be very good timing. Timing is not just reacting quickly to a need or problem. Really good timing is being ahead of these problems and addressing or even preventing them before they become problems. Gaining a reputation for this kind of timing will help get others to listen to you in the future more carefully.

6. **Look for unintended consequences.** Unintended consequences cannot always be avoided, but giving things some good thought and consideration about possible unanticipated reactions or outcomes can be time well spent. Not rushing into a decision but taking even just a few moments to think about unintended consequences can sometimes prevent you and your company from shooting yourselves in the foot.

    As a truly engaged leader, you can play a big part in helping the organization better understand possible unintended consequences beforehand. You need to not only have this perspective but help others see things in a similar way. This is a voice that the organization needs to hear. By thinking through the impact that the organization's actions and decisions may have on employees' feelings, you can help everyone understand the need for more employee engagement. As a simple example, would implementing an aggressive across-the-board salary reduction as a means of cost cutting in reaction to market conditions have the unintended result of a mass exodus of the best employees directly to the competition? You need the ability to recognize the potential for this type of unintended consequence, to voice the concern, and to offer alternatives to address the concern without becoming the company's "Chicken Little," predicting doom in every difficult decision that the organization wants to make.

This requires making intelligent, well-thought-out arguments originating from an engaging perspective.

7. **Anticipate power plays.** You are the victim of a power play when someone uses personal or organizational leverage to get others to oppose something you may have suggested. Why this occurs is not often clear, but sometimes it is a form of cutthroat competition by an ambitious coworker or petty retribution for being perceived as "going around" or "showing up" someone. Once you are outmaneuvered by a power play, it may be politically difficult or even impossible to persuade other key influencers in the organization to back your position. The best thing you can do is to anticipate these power plays and try to prevent them from occurring in the first place.

   Predicting how certain people with the organizational power and savvy to effectively accomplish a power play may react to a particular subject or issue may be easier than you think. People usually are fairly consistent in their behavior. You probably already know how certain people will react in given situations based on your past history with these individuals. In these circumstances, you might try to outflank the potential saboteur by pre-vetting your idea with others and getting them on board before the saboteur has a chance to undermine your idea. Such an approach may be effective, but it is both risky and inviting of an escalation in hostilities.

   A better approach might be to try diffusing the potential for sabotage by winning your potential saboteur over before presenting your idea to the others, approaching the individual in private and explaining your motivation and reasoning for wanting to do something ahead of time. You should acknowledge that you understand and respect their feelings and ask them to at least listen to your ideas, explaining why it would be to everyone's advantage. This approach dampens fear that you or, more importantly, your ideas are threatening their position or authority. You might just find less opposition to your ideas, and that your voice gets heard much better as a result than just waiting for the inevitable behind-the-scenes opposition.

8. **Lobby your concept.** Similar to the previous suggestion, you should also try to gain as many allies for your proposal or position as possible—even those who you would not expect to oppose your idea. Make sure that everyone understands what are the reasons and rationales for your position and why it is important that they support the concept or idea. Be sure to also express this from their perspective by pointing out how their interests may be best served as well. The more allies you have on the particular subject, the better your chances of not only getting your ideas heard but accepted.

9. **Be willing to compromise.** Life is full of compromises, and sometimes you may need to give up some of the things you initially hoped to change or implement in your leadership role. Compromising does not necessarily mean that you give up your core principles or the concepts you feel are important. Rather it means that you have to be realistic about what you can influence or change at least at the moment. There are always a number of different perspectives and agendas that all must be served in any organization. The key decision makers need to listen to everyone's ideas and proposals and make difficult decisions that will not usually please everyone.

Other times you may need to negotiate with business associates and give up some of the things you hoped to achieve to gain support of at least part of your overall objective. This is all part of the give and take of dealing with others in the business world. Being flexible enough to compromise when it is the best strategy and work with others to achieve acceptable solutions to everyone will make your voice more readily heard by others.

And when it is you who possesses the upper hand, using your own superior strength in a particular situation to force your will without compromise may be short-sighted. There will come a time when the shoe is on the other foot, and you can expect similar treatment from the person you have "stuck it to."

10. **Lose graciously.** You need to accept the fact that you are not always going to get what you want or even get your voice heard in many situations and simply just move on to your next challenge. Again, that is all part of business and life. It is important that you handle these situations professionally. Do not take it personally or attack those you feel successfully opposed you. The worst thing you can do in such situations is to damage your working relationships permanently as you will inevitably need the support of these individuals again in the future. This will make your voice less likely to be heard next time. Also, unless you are truly committed enough to follow through, do not go for broke in a last-ditch effort to gain support for an issue by making dramatic outbursts that you will regret afterward such as, "I'm not going to keep working for an organization that won't listen to me!" If you use such threats as a tactic, you might just get what you asked for and find yourself figuratively "out the door" when you lose your ability to influence others.

Chapter 1: Discussion Points

Going back to the introduction, who in your organization do you think would have been the one given a seat in the lifeboat under these terrible circumstances?

> ➤ Do you think experience is valued in your organization? If not, why not? If so, how do you show it is valued?

Does your organization have an issue with the engagement levels of its long-term workers?

> ➤ What kind of institutional signals are they receiving?

> ➤ Are you doing anything to promote higher levels of engagement in this group?

> ➤ Are stereotypes influencing your treatment of or expectations from this group?

The chapter discussed the concept of the "soft stuff" being the hardest to manage at times.

> ➤ Looking back at the operator training issue, what do you think should have been done to prevent this soft-stuff type problem from occurring? What do you think caused the failure to meaningfully include the older workers? How might they have become engaged?

> ➤ What are some examples in your organization of soft-stuff problems causing seemingly unexplained problems?

How well do you manage change as a leader?

> ➤ Do you agree with the statement in this chapter, "Most leaders support change but probably prefer that it happen someplace else in the organization."

- Be honest with yourself: does this reflect your own feelings about change?

- If so, what are you going to do to change your attitude about engagement and change?

The chapter also talked about removing barriers to employee engagement in an organization.

➤ Do any of these types of barriers exist in your organization?
- If so, how can these barriers be removed?

- Do you currently have policies in your organization that inhibit engagement for your older workers?

- Are there signs that your company is a *habitualized organization* as described in this chapter?

This chapter did not mean to imply that all of an organization's habits or cycles are a problem. Many do serve a very productive function. The point is that some of these may be counterproductive and may need to be challenged, such as the example of the top talent search process at that particular company.

➤ Do any such organizational cycles or habits exist in your organization that are actually counterproductive to their intended goals or purpose?

- Do they exist at least in part because they are either perceived or actual "sacred cows" of someone in your organization?

- How can these organizational cycles be broken in your organization?

Finally, going back to the story of the Case of the Untrained Experienced Operators, what do you think the plant manager said to the CEO when he called him to tell him what the real cause of the production problems that virtually everyone in the organizations had been trying to solve for those past few months? What do you think the CEO said to this plant manager?

➤ How would you have liked to have been that plant manager making this call?

➤ Hopefully, the lessons presented in this book will help prevent you from ever having to make such a call ever in your career!

Chapter 2

The New Age of Employee Engagement

As we noted in our Preface to the book, the aging of the Baby Boomers is a double-sided issue for today's employers. On the one hand, many workers who might have retired early or at least by the time they reached a company's normal retirement age now feel they have to or want to continue working beyond that age. Today's reality is that many if not most employees may no longer stop working at the traditional retirement age.

On the other hand, many employers may find it necessary to encourage continued employment instead of retirement for at least their highly skilled workers. A recent news article, headlined "Battered U.S. oil firms scramble to delay looming retirement wave," described the potential mass exodus of skilled Baby Boomers hired in the 1970s that would result in the possible loss of half of the oil industry workforce in the next five to seven years. The situation is worse in some industries, like oil and gas that have limited their hiring over a long period, thereby creating a large experience gap in their workforce. As a result, many companies are taking steps to retain their older workers even during general workforce reductions, such as offering them more flexible work arrangements designed to encourage them to continue working.

With 10,000 Baby Boomers each day reaching the age of 65, this is becoming a significant issue and one that could potentially impact almost every employer for the foreseeable future.

Given the reality that many employees will continue working whether by choice or not, wouldn't it be preferable to find ways to keep them fully engaged contributors?

The future can provide real benefits for your organization by virtue of the fact that employees are beginning to extend their careers. The key is being prepared to take full advantage of this increased career longevity.

This career longevity will put increasing pressure on employers to adapt not only many of their compensation and benefits programs but the way they think about the employment relationship itself. It is vitally important that employers make an attempt to understand the wants, needs, and motivations of their older workers. Employees will have different needs as they enter the final phase of their careers. The biggest problem is addressing the mindset of both parties that employees' employment will come to a natural conclusion when they reach a particular age. This simply is no longer always going to be the case. As the employee longevity curve moves out perhaps even a decade or more, virtually every employment process and system in the organization will need to adapt to this shift. How to capitalize on the talent of older workers who will be working longer should be a top priority of every organization. This will require finding ways to keep these older workers not just employed but fully engaged. Organizations must become just as invested in the career management of their older workers as they are in developing the careers of their younger workers.

The Benefits of Working Longer

The benefits of working longer are not just economic, even if this may be the driving force behind this significant societal change. Although working longer may intuitively seem like bad news, there are many potential positive aspects of this new reality. There is evidence that working longer can be beneficial to one's health, both physically and mentally. Working longer can actually be a factor in delaying or even avoiding such illnesses as Alzheimer's or dementia by keeping older workers' minds active and challenged. Other diseases caused by a more sedentary lifestyle such as heart problems or diabetes may also be prevented or decreased by continuing to work longer. Many other "old age" ailments may be alleviated by a more active (i.e., working) lifestyle.

Older workers stay socially connected with their coworkers and others they come in contact with in the course of their jobs. Working longer provides daily purpose, goals, and sense of accomplishment for older workers. They maintain their skill sets and ability to manage their lives independently longer. Older workers may take better care of themselves so that they can remain productively employed. They also feel less of a burden on others and more in control of their own lives. When you think about it, how could having employees remaining active, contributing, energized, and healthier longer into their careers and lives not be a good thing for everyone?

There are many economic advantages to working longer, both short and long term. Every day one works past his or her "normal" retirement age, there is a greater economic benefit to the individual. Not only is the employee not yet dipping into his or her retirement savings but hopefully enhancing these benefits by continuing to save, and this financial advantage grows exponentially. Just working a few years longer than originally planned can have a significant financial impact on one's eventual retirement. This is good for both the employee and their employer.

Delaying one's Social Security benefits from a reduced early benefit to a full allocation at a later normal retirement date or beyond can also have significant future retirement income benefits. Employees can better maintain their current lifestyle for a longer period of time, assuming that their income will be reduced in retirement as is typically the case.

We know that employers are increasingly jettisoning company-sponsored pension and retirement medical plans due to the increasing cost of providing them. In fact, some companies have had their very existence threatened by the weight of these obligations. If workers work longer, some of these financial burdens may decrease. For example, employer sponsored retiree health care programs will be providing benefits for a shorter period of time. Employers who sponsor retiree health programs will have fewer of the very expensive pre-Medicare retirees in their retiree health plans. Employers will reduce their future legacy costs relating to pensions and other retiree benefits for employees who are no longer contributing to the bottom line.

So too, older workers will maintain their active employee benefit coverage, which is also good for them. If an older worker does become ill during active employment, there may be short-term and longer-term disability programs available that retirees would not have had in retirement.

Age Bias Concerns

The shift in the age demographics of the future workforce gives a new dimension to the problem of age discrimination. There are many laws prohibiting various forms of bias in employment regardless if it is unconscious or not. These laws are meant to protect persons from being discriminated against based on various characteristics, e.g., race, sex, or age. Of these various protected characteristics, age appears unique because it seems that age may logically be linked to a person's ability, aspirations, or expectations, while other protected characteristics such as race or sex or national origin have no rational connection to such things.

For example, it has been generally true that most workers who are 62 or older expect to leave the company voluntarily within the next five years. Would it make sense to send a 62-year-old worker to an executive MBA program designed to prepare them for advancement to a senior-level job five to ten years out in their career? There could be no logical rationale for excluding someone from such an opportunity based on their sex, race, or national origin. But because age and length of expected service are so directly linked, one could argue that it would be a waste of resources to make such an investment in an older worker. On the other hand, one could argue that arbitrarily excluding older workers from consideration for such a career development opportunity based on age is clear-cut age discrimination.

Making the problem of dealing openly with the issue of age in today's workplace more difficult is the perception that even talking to your older employees about their long-term career plans can be problematic. With our society's increasing propensity for employment-related lawsuits, it is, to say the least, a very delicate issue to even bring up the topic of an employee's expected retirement date. Even broaching such a topic can be risky business as it could be considered as evidence of age bias in an age-discrimination lawsuit. Raising the subject of retirement with an older employee can be viewed as encouraging or even pressuring him to retire. With this trend toward extended career longevity inevitably continuing in the future, it should be expected that even more legislation protecting the rights of older workers will become part of the legal landscape surrounding this subject.

This fear of legal claims places a barrier between the employer and the older employee in frankly discussing career aspirations and alternatives that may both recognize the realities of the employee's limited time horizon and likely very limited potential for further career advancement. What is needed is to address the needs of both employer and employee finding ways to keep the employee as engaged and productive as possible during the final phase of his or her career.

If this is indeed the case, it will be ever more important to find ways to appropriately enter into a dialog with older employees about their plans to continue working longer in their career. Employers and their older workers need to have this meaningful dialog so that they both can plan for these extended careers in the most productive manner possible for everyone. The best approach is to ask older employees about their career goals and aspirations rather than their retirement plans. Obviously, you may want to discuss with your legal and human resource advisors for guidance on how to best approach these important discussions in your organization.

There are many reasons why older employees may need to continue working longer into their careers in the future than ever before, many of which have to do with changes in their financial health as the following example illustrates:

Still Working

Jerry Hagans had worked for the same company for his entire career, which spanned over three decades. Jerry had always dreamed of retiring in his early 60s to enjoy his family and favorite hobbies, which included playing golf every chance he could get. It never really occurred to Jerry when he started out in his career that he might not be able to achieve this goal. He thought if he just worked hard and could progress through the ranks of the company, he would be ready financially for retirement at age 62. But things have a way of changing for reasons over which you have little or no control.

The company Jerry worked for had been bought and sold a number of times during the last half of his career, bringing many changes to the employee benefit plans including the loss of the company's defined retirement benefit plan. At his original company, the defined retirement benefit pension plan provided a guaranteed set amount each month to retirees based on an employee's age and service. Today, all the newest owners were offering retirees was a 401(k) retirement plan. This changed Jerry's prospects of an early retirement as he was falling woefully short of his financial goal to be able to retire comfortably at the age he had hoped to retire.

So this left Jerry still working after what he had hoped was already a career lifetime of employment—something neither he nor his employer expected. Jerry's career plan was always based on progressing through the typical management ranks and finally reaching a certain level in the organization that would take him to a comfortable retirement, but this wasn't happening. Now, working for this newest acquiring company, he was at a level in the organization somewhat short of his career goal with seemingly no future promotions ahead of him for whatever number of years he would continue to need to work. This was throwing everything off not just for Jerry, but also for his employer as it became apparent that his natural attrition into retirement wasn't going to occur as the new company was anticipating. Neither was prepared for this scenario. Both the company and Jerry felt somehow trapped by their situation.

Coming to grips with this scenario is something that is occurring more and more often in organizations today. Neither employers nor older employees needing to remain employed longer than either expected are adequately prepared for the changes that are occurring in the workplace today and will continue into the future. Anticipating these changes and beginning to take action today to address the increasing longevity of careers can make this experience not only less stressful but mutually beneficial for both employers and employees.

The Engagement Formula for Older Workers: Ability × Motivation = Employee Engagement

This simple formula clearly defines what employee engagement is really all about for older employees. First, employees must have the ability to be able to perform their jobs at a level expected and desired by the organization. This isn't possible if they don't have the skills, training, direction, equipment, etc., necessary to perform their jobs correctly. Providing these *ability* factors in this engagement formula is the responsibility of the organization, and this is especially true in the case of older employees. As an engaged leader, you need to be your employees' advocate to ensure that what is being expected of them is reasonable and fair. It simply is not fair to expect an employee of any age to perform his or her job at an engaged level without providing these necessary resources. All the engagement efforts in the world won't make much of a difference in the end if these factors are not addressed.

Any perceived deficiency on the part of an older, experienced worker with regard to the ability side of the engagement equation may well be based on false presumptions about their unwillingness to update their skills or accept change. Their years of experience and knowledge typically more than qualify them to perform well, assuming they have been provided the training and resources required for continued success in their jobs. The issue may be that they haven't been provided these developmental opportunities.

Motivation is the second part of the formula and is different from ability. An older employee may have the ability to perform his or her job but not be motivated to do so as was the case in the previous story. In many cases, employees like Jerry lose their drive and desire to perform their jobs at a higher level. They have become *disengaged.* There are many reasons why employees get to this state of mind. Many times older workers are simply responding to the way they believe they are being valued or more specifically, the lack of value they perceive their employer currently sees in them. They may feel that their time has passed, that younger seemingly more capable employees are pushing them out the door, or that they no longer can keep up with the fast pace of today's workplace. This is the part of the equation that needs to change the most in the future.

Changing the mindset that many employers have about their older workers is not easy and takes time. Recognizing and addressing the career expectations and needs of older workers can make them more motivated to become or stay engaged in their jobs and careers far longer. Many of the reasons associated with older workers' disengagement are based on a lack of trust. This mistrust goes both ways in the organization between employers and older workers. Regaining or even establishing trust between these employees and the organization is the key to employee engagement of older workers. This is no easy task. Trust is one of those things that takes a long time to build but can be destroyed very quickly. Becoming an engaging leader to your older workers is perhaps the best way to gain the trust of those who report to you. Getting involved with and caring about these employees is the first step.

Ability and motivation are both closely tied to trust. Providing the resources for older employees to be able to continue to perform their jobs demonstrates trust. The organization trusts that there will be a return on this investment in their older employees and that they will be motivated to perform their jobs to their greatest ability. These employees appreciate being given the resources to improve their skills and add value to the organization and to their careers. Motivation on the part of employees to utilize their ability is based on the trust that there will be something in it for them. If they think that all the gains are one-sided in favor of the organization, then their motivation to utilize their ability will be diminished. Discovering the reason for a lack of motivation sometimes takes some extra effort as was the case with David White in the following story:

Motivating David

David White was frustrated with his job and his career. It seemed despite his many years of experience as a systems analyst and extensive knowledge about the company's computer systems that he was no longer thought of very highly in his company. It wasn't always this way. At one time, he felt that his talent and ability was being recognized. He loved coming to work. But things had changed. He felt left behind, more like an aging athlete, once important to the team but now relegated to riding the bench. He seemed to be just going through the motions of his job, getting what needed to be done but not accomplishing much more.

His boss, Frank Lindsey, had noticed this and was becoming concerned about David. He knew that David could contribute so much more but was not sure how to motivate him to perform to his potential. Frank had discussed these concerns with David during his past few annual performance reviews, but nothing ever seemed to change as a result. Although, David didn't know it, there was even some discussion about terminating his employment with the company despite his many years of service as plans were being made for a reduction-in-force due to declining business. This was something that Frank did not want to see happen since he had a great deal of respect for David and his potential to again really make a contribution in his job. Frank decided to try one more time to understand exactly what was holding David back and causing his continuing mediocre performance. He arranged a meeting with David to discuss this problem the following week.

When Monday morning arrived, David reported to his office. "David, as I have been telling you for some time now, I am concerned about your current job performance. It's obviously not a matter of ability in your case; you just don't seem to be motivated any more to do more than just the minimum. That's what is so frustrating to not only me but to others in the organization as well," Frank began the discussion.

"It's like I have told you, Frank. Things have changed so much in the past few years. I still know how to do this job, but I don't seem to know how to deal with this new structure around here. I don't know who I am supposed to be dealing with and where I am supposed to go to get direction. I know that you try to be of help, but you are gone so much of the time on that new project that I don't feel I have access to you when I need it," David complained.

"I am sorry if you don't feel you have access to me when you need it. The reality is that I am out of the country much of the time, so getting access to me is going to continue to be a problem at least until this project is completed. But I don't think that is really the problem, as we have discussed this before. I still think that it is more than that. Could you help me better understand why you feel the way you do?" Frank probed.

"Well, this may seem silly to you, but one of the things that really bothers me the most is when I quietly come up with a great solution to a serious problem and don't get so much as a pat on the back for it. This has been happening more and more lately. That really hurts," David candidly answered.

"No, it doesn't sound silly to me, and I don't remember you mentioning this to me before. Why haven't you brought this up in our previous conversations about your performance?" Frank asked a bit perplexed by this revelation.

"I guess I didn't want to seem like I wasn't a team player or something like that. I'm always happy to help out the younger guys, but it really bothers me to see others continuing to get credit for my expertise. For example, I came up with the idea that the most recent big systems problem might be fixed with a simple software patch instead of replacing all the hardware. We saved a bundle, and we were back online in a fraction of the time. But nobody seemed to get the message that this was my idea. The new younger guys seem to be much better at getting themselves in the spotlight than I am anymore," David answered. "I used to feel that my contributions would be recognized without my having to blow my own horn. It doesn't seem to work that way anymore. It makes me wonder what the use is of going the extra mile when it doesn't get me anywhere."

"I honestly didn't know anything about your involvement in that problem. In fact, this is the first I have heard that you were even involved in finding that solution," Frank said.

"That doesn't exactly make me feel any better!" David lamented.

"No, I am sure it doesn't. We need to fix this problem. Do you have any suggestions about how this could be addressed and how you can get the recognition you deserve?" Frank asked, reminding himself that David usually does have the answer to most problems.

"Well, if it would be OK with you," David began, "I would like to give you regular updates on what I am involved in and the contributions I am making. I think you will be surprised about just how many people do come to me behind the scenes for advice and direction concerning the most difficult problems that we face on a regular basis. I don't just tell others what needs to be done; I also help them get it done correctly. I could email these updates so you are kept current on these things even when you are traveling. Maybe that way you could make sure that the right people know about my contributions."

"Yes, that would be fine. That way I can forward these updates to my boss as well. Why don't you start this week," Frank suggested.

David left the meeting more enthusiastic about his job than he had been for a long time.

It is this combination of ability and motivation that results in true employee engagement. The secret to this employee engagement formula is ensuring that employees of all ages have the training and skills needed to perform their jobs and are motivated to perform their jobs with a high level of engagement. As this story illustrates, this can be especially important to an older worker such as David White who may be feeling a bit insecure about his perceived value to the organization even to the point where it begins to affect his motivation to perform his job. This is not a simple goal to accomplish. It involves many factors and variables to make this workplace culture possible. In this case, it apparently turned out to be a simple matter of ensuring that David received the recognition he felt he deserved for him to begin to become engaged again in his job.

Chapter 2: Discussion Points

Is your organization currently experiencing a shift in the average retirement age of your employees?

> ➢ If so, what has been the change in the average age of retirees?

> ➢ What impact is this having on your organization?

> ➢ Do you currently think of this change as an opportunity or a challenge? Why?

> ➢ If your organization hasn't yet seen this shift in age of employees, do you expect this to occur in the future? How long do you think this shift might take to begin to feel its impact in your organization?

> ➢ What are you doing to help make this shift in the age demographic of your workforce successful from both your employees' perspective and the organization's.

Has your organization thought about this shift in retirement ages from your employees' perspective? How so?

Have you experienced any motivational issues with older employees?

> ➢ What do you think is the cause of these issues?

> ➢ Which of these issues might be caused or aggravated by the organization in some way?

> ➢ What have you done to address these issues?

> ➢ What can you do differently in the future to address these issues?

How effectively do you think David's manager dealt with the motivational issues he was experiencing in this story?

> ➢ How well do you think this manager pursued what was really bothering David?
>
> > – What did the manager do to discover the real reason David was becoming disengaged? How effectively do you think he responded to David's first explanation for the reason he was feeling the way he did?
>
> ➢ What do you think would have happened if this manager had not found the real reason David was feeling demotivated?
>
> ➢ Do you believe that David will be more motivated concerning his job after this discussion? Why or why not?
>
> ➢ What might have you done differently in this situation if you were David's manager?

Chapter 3

Sexagenarians in the Workplace

Don't worry: having sexagenarians in your workplace is not a violation of your harassment policy! To the contrary: sexagenarians are those whose age is between 60 and 69 years old, and their numbers in the workplace are going to be growing significantly. Our society is already reflecting the reality that successful people are often not ready for retirement when they have reached what used to be considered retirement age. Think about all of the politicians, rock stars, and actors who keep working beyond their 60s. Why shouldn't your employees? The reality is that employees may even work till they are 80 or even further into the future. Hey, if Mick Jagger can rock on into his 70s, why can't your employees continue to be productive in their jobs at that age? The reality is that your employees can still rock on in their careers; you just need to give them the opportunity.

Healthier lifestyles of today are slowing the aging process. Medical advancements are enabling us to live and be active longer. The hands of time are being pushed backward in the workplace, and the number of productive working years of employees is increasing.

There is a new employment timeline emerging that will become the norm in the future. To put these changes in perspective, shown below is the traditional timeline that most employees up until now have typically followed throughout their careers:

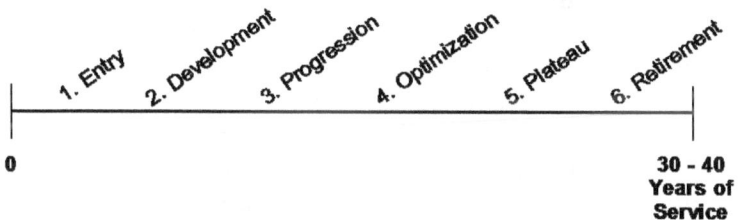

Figure 1. Traditional Career Timeline

Employees typically begin their careers in an entry-level position, basically learning their profession in either a formal or an informal system, gaining the experience and knowledge needed for future advancement. As they develop in their careers, it becomes more apparent what each individual's future potential may be to move up in the organization. As employees begin to hone the skills needed to be successful in their careers, they begin to progress. The level they eventually progress to will be determined by a myriad of factors, including the employee's own motivation and aspirations. Sometime in everyone's career, they are going to optimize their talents and abilities. This optimization may or may not be apparent from the onset. It may be a slow, gradual ascent, or it may be more immediately apparent, depending on the position the individual has reached during his or her career progression. Career optimization typically leads to a plateau of one's career. This is the point in one's career from where he or she realistically would not expect to progress.

For many employees, the reaching of this plateau in their careers coincides with their personal aspirations and desires. Their transition out of the workforce through retirement occurs naturally, accompanied by a sense of satisfaction for having had a good career and hope for an equally satisfying retirement.

For some employees, the reaching of this plateau occurs prematurely from their perspective. Such individuals may not believe or accept they have reached the final plateau in their careers, but the decision makers in the organization might have already made this determination. This leads to frustration, resentment, and, eventually, disengagement. They continue working until they retire with a sense of bitterness, or even worse, they are involuntarily terminated.

What is changing is how long this overall timeline takes to come to fruition. Regardless of which of these scenarios plays itself out in any given employee's career, traditionally a career has spanned 30 or even 40 years, typically ending sometime between ages 60 and 65. Employers were able to lend predictability to this process by designing their retirement plans to foster transition of their older workers having reached their career plateau to retirement, a planned funded expense that has been part of their overall business plan. What is occurring now is going to knock this model on its ear. Employees may not nicely fit into this model for all the reasons previously mentioned.

What is needed is an understanding that the lifespan of the average career has changed, probably forever. The lifespan of careers, like the average lifespan of workers, is growing Employees' productive years—the years before they reach the final career plateau—are increasing and so too are both their need and desire to remain working longer into their now extended lives. To effectively respond to this change, employers need to rethink their perception of the average career lifespan. No longer can or should they expect nearly all of their employees to be naturally planning on retirement at traditional ages. Employees will be in the workplace for the longer haul, perhaps decades beyond even what Social Security currently considers a normal retirement age. Are employers ready for such a shift in the age in their workforce? The golden age of early mass retirement is gone, replaced by the reality that workers will want to remain employed much longer, perhaps literally for a lifetime. Lifetime employment may become more than merely an expression but a reality in the future. The concept of the presumptive retiree may no longer have any meaning. Planned career obsolescence is no longer a viable strategy. The 30- to 40-year career plan is gone, replaced by the 40-plus-year career. Even the concept of one's career is changing as one's job will occupy an even greater portion of people's lives as it extends into their golden *working* years.

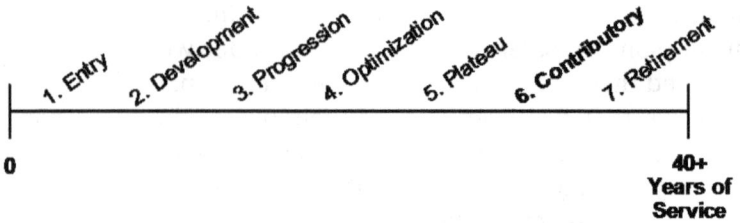

Figure 2. The New Career Timeline

As this model illustrates in Figure 2, there is a new career timeline beginning to emerge that will shift the expectations of both employers and older workers. A new phase of employment will begin to exist that can be called *contributory*. This will become a distinct phase of employment completely different than the traditional phases described above. What is unique about this contributory phase is that it occurs at the point when employees would traditionally retire. At this point in employees' lives, the employees have potentially both different needs and contributions to make to the organization than earlier in their careers. They may no longer be focused on career progression or even promotion, but more concerned about job security, continuing to make a contribution, and even personal fulfillment. These employees want to be provided with opportunities to utilize their experience and talents in other ways more conducive to their current needs. This may require more creative thinking on the part of employers to find ways to maximize the talents and abilities of their older workers entering this new phase of their employment. Many of the traditional aspects of employment—such as benefit program designs, working schedules, physical work locations, reporting relationships, job designs, and other job related requirements—may need to be adapted to accommodate these older workers.

Staying Younger by Working Longer

This model reflects a slowing down of the career aging process and a further cheating, or at least fending off, of Father Time. It is redefining the concept of career in terms of expectations and longevity. Employees are now staying younger by working longer. By extending the productive years, the traditional career-stage model is no longer valid. No longer can employers expect virtually all of their older employees to wind down their careers in their late 50s or early 60s. Indeed, for many employers, perpetuation of the traditional career trajectory could actually be considered a threat due to the loss of not readily replaceable talents and skills. Many employees are now in for the longer haul concerning their careers. As the average career starts to extend into one's late 60s or 70s, changes need to occur to adjust to this shift in working longevity as illustrated in the following story:

Falling Off the Promotion List

Laverne Johnson had worked for ACME Engineering Incorporated for nearly all of her adult working life after being hired directly from college as an entry-level engineer. She had progressed rather quickly through the engineering ranks as a young engineer after being identified early on as top talent by the company's management development committee. Laverne's career progressed into more and more responsible management roles, supervising departments and eventually an entire division of this medium-sized engineering firm. Laverne was highly respected by everyone and never seemed to have too many concerns about her future career development and growth with the company.

That is, until she reached her late 50s when she began to notice that she seemed to be no longer in the mix for promotions to positions that she still had an interest in aspiring to as part of what she believed to be her continuing career progression. She asked her boss many times why she seemed to no longer make any of the promotion lists like she did in the past. All she got were vague answers that she was well-suited for her current role and no changes were planned for her at this

---

time. This was both very curious and upsetting to Laverne. She felt that she was continuing to perform at the same or even better level than she had ever before in her long and distinguished career with ACME. She suspected that she knew the answer to her questions, and in fact, her suspicions were correct.

Laverne had fallen victim to the inference at ACME, based on its past experience, that once someone reaches a certain age in his or her career, promotion is unlikely regardless of how well they were performing their current job or their qualifications to be promoted to the next level. The underlying rationale was that at some point in one's career that the employee in effect becomes a "short-timer" and it would be unreasonable and unrealistic to consider them part of the company's longer-term plans. Laverne realized this and, at some level even accepted it, albeit with a certain level of resentment. What bothered Laverne even more was the fact that her performance evaluations were also being affected by this change, and this had an impact both on her annual raise as well as her bonus, which represented a large portion of her total compensation package.

For many reasons, Laverne wanted to continue working even after reaching her normal retirement age even though she was one of few in the company who still had a grandfathered defined pension benefit as well as money put away in the 401(k) company-sponsored plan. She still worried if she had enough to support her and her husband for their expected extended lifetimes.

Although Laverne wanted to continue working as she approached this stage of her life and career, in her heart of hearts, she was also concerned about her ability to continue to perform at the levels she had during her entire career to date. Her job required many extra hours to meet the ever-increasing demands of managing an entire engineering division of the company not to mention extensive travel, often globally. She worried about remaining competitive in the fast-paced, demanding environment of today as she aged. Laverne had always thrived on the challenges of balancing a demanding workload and the responsibilities of her family life, but she was seeing the signs that she was less able, and possibly less willing, to maintain the same level of intensity and effort she had as a younger woman. Laverne's career goals and objectives were beginning to change.

Truth be told, at this point, she was becoming less concerned about career advancement and more about continued job security. Laverne had always just taken for granted that she had job security as long as she worked for the company. Now, she was less sure. She previously had been much more focused on other goals such as advancement, recognition, and excelling in her job, which she did. Although, she was still interested in these things, she was beginning to think about them differently. What she really wanted was to be able to continue working as long as she felt she could make a contribution but not exactly in the same capacity as earlier in her career. She did not want to lose all chance of advancement or to see her performance rating fall simply based on some presumption about when she would retire. Laverne wanted to be provided career-extending opportunities, but not necessarily through placement in jobs on the promotion ladder applicable to younger workers. Rather, she wished for meaningful opportunities to contribute to the company in ways more reflective of her current stage in her work and personal lives.

Laverne was at the contributory stage of her career. She was far from ready to stop working and retire. She looked forward to new challenges that her career could offer, but in different ways than earlier in her career. She needed a role in the organization in which she could share the wealth of knowledge and experience she had gained during her many years with the company, but in a capacity that would be valuable to the company and appropriate for someone in the final stages of her working career.

The president of ACME knew Laverne very well as they had worked together for many years. Laverne's situation became a wakeup call for the president. He began to realize that the traditional career progression process in the company did not fit the needs of older workers desiring to remain employed beyond their expected retirement ages. The president began to rethink the talent review processes in place in the organization and how it eventually impacted and, perhaps more accurately, failed older workers. He realized that a different career progression process needed to be implemented to address the needs of older workers desiring to not only remain employed but to continue to progress in their careers far beyond what was traditionally expected to be the end of their careers and began to implement these programs.

As this story illustrates, there should be an awaking in every organization about the needs of the expanding group of older workers, especially those whose desire it is to continue working longer and productively in extended careers.

In the past, despite the potential for age discrimination claims by passed-over workers, ACME's pragmatic promotion philosophy might have worked fairly well as it was readily accepted by employees approaching their normal retirement ages whose focus inevitably turned to exiting the company rather than remaining employed for any length of time. They were satisfied going into wind-down mode as they looked forward to their well-earned retirement.

But today, as Laverne's case illustrates, this presumptive retirement model is changing. No longer can it be presumed that employees are planning to retire at what formerly was expected to be their normal retirement age. Nor can they be expected to simply begin to fade off into their sunsets of retirement when they reach their late 50s or early to mid-60s. Many employees in their 50s and 60s are now in it for the long haul with the expectation of years, if not decades, of continued employment ahead of them. Not having enough career "runway"; i.e., not having enough time left in an employee's career before retirement to justify an investment in any future career development, will no longer be a valid excuse for excluding such employees from career advancement opportunities. Runways need to be extended to accommodate the realities of the Baby Boomer generation as well as later generations.

Chapter 3: Discussion Points

Do you agree with the traditional career timeline, as shown in Figure 1 of this chapter? If not, what would you change?

> ➢ Although not specifically shown in Figure 1, there will be differences in the amount of time an employee takes to progress from one stage of this model to the next. For instance, the optimization stage may last for many years of an employee's career, or the progression stage may take relatively little time to complete. How has your career timeline progressed in terms of time in each of these phases as you have progressed according to this model?

> ➢ Do you agree that this traditional timeline will change as a result of shifting age demographics of our workforces in the future? Why or why not?

> ➢ In what ways do see this changing?

Reviewing Figure 2, there is a new career phase introduced—contributing. Do you agree that this should be identified as a distinct career phase? Why or why not?

> ➢ Or do you think that many job incumbents working longer in their careers simply just want to remain in their jobs and not be treated any differently than their younger counterparts? Why or why not?

> ➢ Or is it possible that even older employees not yet wanting to be treated any differently at the present time may someday want to be considered more in this mature career phase? Why do you believe this way?

In reading the story in this chapter about Laverne Johnson, are there aspects of her story that may relate to how your own organization views employees approaching or reaching their expected normal retirement ages?

> ➤ Does the term *presumptive retirement* apply to the current thinking in your organization? If yes, what could be the possible problems or issues that this type of thinking causes for your organization?

> ➤ How important do you think the president of the company's involvement was in changing the way the company viewed its older workers such as Laverne?

> ➤ Does your organization need to consider a different career progression process? If so, read on as the following chapters will help you better understand what this new career model for older employees should look like and how to get started implementing it.

Chapter 4

Greyforce

We are in the midst of the creation of a new multi-generational workforce that will include at least one more generations of workers than has been typical in the past. In the past, as a new generation of 18- to 25-year-old workers entered the workforce, the generation of 55- to 65-year-old workers transitioned out of the workforce. Now the generation gap between active workers is widening. The age and corresponding generational differences in perspectives between the youngest and oldest workers will be greater than they have ever been. Today's workforce—and even more so, the workforce of tomorrow—will include both the ultra-savvy newest generation steeped in the latest technologies seemingly from birth and the aging Baby Boomer generation as well. These aging Baby Boomers will be working well into what may be called their "silver years"—that is, the time of life when someone is no longer really a "middle-ager" but not yet a "golden-ager." This is what may be called the emergence of the *Greyforce* in the workplace of the future. While the Baby Boom generation is leading this trend, and their sheer numbers make it a scary prospect, this phenomenon likely will continue beyond the natural attrition of the Boomers because, with the loss of traditional pensions and the increase in lifespan, every generation will want or need to work longer than the previous one. This shift to a workforce that includes an increasing number of older workers has already begun as more and more aging Boomers decide to defer their retirements either of their own accord or at the behest of their employers. It is introducing a new dimension in organizations and on their cultures. Organizations need to respond to what is happening and to prepare for the even larger Greyforce of the future.

The workers in generations following the Baby Boomers will be far less likely than Boomers to work for a single employer through their entire careers. Instead of counting on retirement being funded by pensions based on years of service with one employer, these workers will base their retirement decisions on their personal savings accumulated during employment with any number of employers. Since they no longer can count on the security of defined benefit pension plans, these workers are even more likely than Boomers to need to extend their careers. In short, the basic challenge of creating value in the employment of an increasingly aged workforce will not go away. It seems destined to increase. Job mobility will not change the basic fact that at some point, most workers will reach the *contributory* career stage, and every employer will need to deal with the wants and needs of such workers.

Traditionally, when employers thought about employees in their 50s and 60s, they were often focusing on succession planning and how they would replace all the years of experience and expertise that would walk out the door when these people left the organization. They assumed that the employees in this age group, with the exception of a few high flyers, were also thinking about their upcoming retirement and settling into the plateau phase, where their career aspirations involved simply working out their time until retirement.

Just think what it would be like if your older employee population in their late 50s who would normally be at least contemplating retirement were instead not even thinking of leaving the organization anytime in the near future. How different would you think about this group of your workforce? Now, think about what the profile of the new Greyforce might look like. Think about a growing segment of your workforce that is over 65 years old. What if this group of highly experienced and knowledgeable employees were still totally committed to their careers, not just marking time until retirement? How might this change the value that you see in this group of employees? The point is that you will likely be confronted with this reality in the future if not already. It is your decision how you utilize this group of employees. You could resist their continued career longevity by treating them as placeholders and looking for ways to incentivize them to leave the organization, or you could find ways to maximize the value to your organization of their experience, knowledge, and continued vitality as long as they wish to remain working. The choice is yours.

Think about the contribution that this Greyforce can provide, but which you may not be capitalizing on today. Your Greyforce collectively has skills, knowledge, abilities, historical information, wisdom, and perhaps other advantages over those with less experience. This is often the most underutilized employee population in organizations. One major reason this group gets marginalized or ignored is the increasingly outmoded presumption that they are primarily focused on preparing themselves for retirement. Stated another way, you may be presuming that they are no longer interested in their jobs. This dismissive mindset is limiting from both the employer's and the employees' perspectives. When their employers act like they presume that members of Greyforce are no longer engaged and just putting in their time until retirement, members may respond in a manner consistent with this mindset: "Why should I care when I apparently am no longer considered relevant?" In some organizations where management totally neglects to foster engagement in their Greyforce workers, this mindset may begin years ahead of time as some older employees seem to retire on the job long before their actual retirement date. And so it has been for decades: a system based on anticipation of natural attrition of older workers at a predictable retirement age results in underutilization and lack of appreciation for the older worker.

Today, we are experiencing a rapid shift in the expectations and needs of older workers. As an employee reaches age 60 or older, he or she is not necessarily thinking about retirement in the near or even distant future. What if this employee is expecting and is able to work another 5, 10, or even 20 more productive years? How does that change the employment relationship for both parties? Obviously, the model that currently exists with the reasonable expectation of retirement at a standard retirement age is no longer going to work effectively. An entirely different employment relationship with supporting systems needs to be developed and implemented.

So what will this new Greyforce expect and how will they behave? What should you expect from this segment of your worker population? Obviously there is no specific stereotype that would accurately depict or represent every older worker in your organization, but there are some commonalities that may exist. For example, members of Greyforce are now working beyond their normal retirement age defined either by Social Security or the organization's definition of a normal retirement date. Greyforce has a desire and possibly the financial need to remain working beyond these normal retirement milestones. And they don't want to just be allowed to remain on the payroll, they want to contribute. But if you treat them as lame ducks, that is eventually what they will become. Their performance will conform to your organization's expectations and the opportunities you provide. If expectations and opportunities are low, performance will be low. Finding the right opportunities to keep members of Greyforce motivated, meaningful contributors during their extend careers will be one of the greatest business challenges employers will face in the future.

This shift in the age of the workforce should not be seen as a negative or a problem. It is an opportunity that you need to be ready to capitalize on. You need to begin to think about the ways in which your organization can adapt to and even capitalize on this shift in workforce demographics. Ask yourself, "What would be the best way to use this experienced and talented group in your future organization?" What gaps do you now have that could be filled by workers of Greyforce? How could your Greyforce create a competitive advantage to you? This is likely a very different perspective than many organizations may have today concerning their aging workforce, which too often is seen more as a liability than an asset. In fact, modern organizations that have come to recognize that diversity is essential to success in today's world should come to view the employment and engagement of Greyforce workers as an important component of that diversity. These topics will be discussed further in the next chapters.

Collaborative Employment

The first thing that you need to do is to take "normal retirement age" out of the organizational vernacular when thinking and talking about your older employees. This is not just to avoid discriminating against older workers, but rather this mindset or perception about the lifespan of a productive career is self-defeating. This is part of what needs to change.

A new mindset about the concept of a "career" is needed to support Greyforce workers. This change begins with redefining the employment relationship at the later stages of employment. This involves both changing career expectations and rethinking the way an employee progresses throughout his or her career in an organization. The career design that has prevailed at least since the end of World War II is essentially based on a cost/benefit progression model of productivity versus time. Employees are essentially hired, trained, promoted/rewarded, and finally receive a retirement significantly financed by their employer(s) during their careers whatever the duration and affiliation with a specific organization. This has been a rewarding arrangement for both parties that has worked fairly well for many decades. Employers got their business needs met, and the employee got the financial security he or she needed, and hopefully some satisfaction from the work they performed. The optimization stage of the career is hopefully a long one for the organization in order to get the greatest return on its investment, but typically not expected to last beyond a certain age.

However, from the employer's perspective, the cost side of this equation has become increasingly unworkable. Employers have been changing part of this employment equation—the part about providing a deferred reward at the end of an employee's career in the form of retirement benefits. The death of the defined retirement benefit has necessitated and will continue to necessitate extension of careers because the financial side of the equation has gotten out of whack from the employees' perspective. Employees feel that they can no longer predict with any degree of comfort what their income will be at the end of their normal working careers, much less whether their savings and other sources of income will be sufficient to see them through the remainder of their lives. The covenant between employers and employees (and, of course, society through the government) that a lifetime of work will result in some modicum of retirement security by the time one reaches one's mid-60s has been breached as a result of force majeure—the unpredicted annihilation of the demographic assumptions upon which the covenant was always based.

What is needed now is a new model for the employment relation: a collaborative employment compact. The current model based on a 30- to 40-year career lifespan is becoming outdated and needs to be replaced to accommodate current realities. What is needed is to find ways to support Greyforce rather than our prevalent practice of off-boarding them, either actually or figuratively, at some pre-determined age.

New Perceptions of Experience

As any young job applicant will tell you, without experience, it seems impossible to get started in one's career. Once some experience is gained, the doors begin to open to many new employment opportunities and this seems to continue over one's career—at least up to a certain point. There comes a time in most people's careers when their lifetime of experience seems to work in the opposite direction. Ironically, at some point on someone's career timeline, they may begin to be perceived as having **too much** experience. Too often, they may be looked at as if they were some sort of outdated technology, something that was once the most current and valued resource available to get the job done but now has reached the end of its useful life and is ready to be replaced by the latest and greatest technology.

But people are not the same as outdated computers. It often makes good business sense to discard a computer and replace it with a newer model. Human beings are obviously much more complicated. With relative ease and relatively low investment by our employers, our experience and knowledge can continue to grow, and we can continue to change to meet new demands and to provide high value to our employer even as we reach and go beyond the point our career would have culminated in an earlier time. The key as illustrated in all of the examples presented in this book is finding ways to unlock this potential in older workers. We need to recognize the great potential that older workers continue to have and the contributions that they can continue to make in the organization as productive and fulfilled employees.

New Challenges of Old Problems

The "value of the experience" of older workers may seem like an outmoded concept in today's world. Indeed, it is fair to say that in at least one sense, experience no longer counts for as much as it once did in the workplace. It used to be that experience performing most jobs made one better able to perform it in comparison to a less experienced worker. Now, due to the pace and effects of technological change and the resultant change in the ways that a particular job might be done, the mere fact that a worker has done a job for a long time does not ensure that he or she will be appreciably more proficient at it than a newbie just out of school. In fact, this phenomenon has made it more likely than before that in hiring or downsizing decisions involving a wide variety of jobs, junior employees might reasonably and objectively be rated as high if not higher than an experienced employee based on their relevant skill sets.

However, experience has other dimensions and benefits that may still count in today's workplace, and it is foolhardy to deprive your organization of them. With experience comes wisdom and judgment, things that can impact the bottom line of any organization. People make better decisions based on the cumulative effect of what they have previously learned through experience. Capitalizing on Greyforce's experience can save an organization enormous sums of money by making better decisions if it only listens to those who possess it.

Today's older workers do not see themselves as has-beens obsessively carping on how things used to be around the workplace in the good old days. They may no longer aspire to be company president, but they want to remain knowledgeable and relevant. At the same time, they take pride in their experience and hope that their unique perspective and the wisdom of their experience will be listened to respectfully, valued appropriately, and acted on accordingly. Which of these alternatives—irrelevant has-beens or vital contributors—becomes a reality in your organization's future will in large measure be determined how your leaders treat older workers. The rest of the organization takes their cue from their leadership.

Insincere and patronizing lip service to Greyforce is a waste of time. It is one thing to just say that the organization respects the opinions of their older workers but another thing to show that it means it. If the leadership of the organization gives the impression that only the younger employees' views really matter, then that is the way everyone will feel. The gold nuggets to be found in the cumulative experience of Greyforce will remain unmined.

Keeping Greyforce Challenged

Older workers need to be challenged in different ways than their younger counterparts. Recognizing this fact is important in keeping older workers engaged. The problem is that the workplace is not usually designed to motivate this segment of an employee population. For example, think about what are the motivators built into most organizational designs.

As illustrated in Figure 3 below, typically the main motivators are promotional opportunities and higher pay. Talk to any younger employee about his or her career goals and this is what you undoubtedly will hear. This is what motivates young and mid-level employees in the workplace.

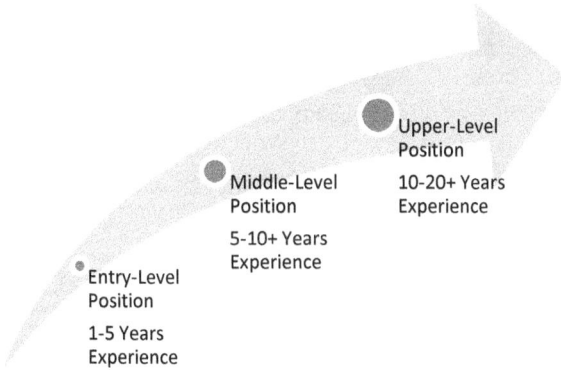

Upper-Level Position

10-20+ Years Experience

Middle-Level Position

5-10+ Years Experience

Entry-Level Position

1-5 Years Experience

Those who may have accepted the fact that they probably will not be promoted during the remainder of their career may still be motivated by the prospect of pay increases based on strong performance. Now what if neither of these goals could be realistically expected to be attained by an employee? What might happen to his or her motivation? This is where you might find your Greyforce workers in your organization. Aside from their personal pride and work ethic, what is there to help them remain fully engaged?

Inclusion in the pool in consideration for promotions, for obvious reasons, is still the primary motivational tool for encouraging talented employees. Realistically, for just as obvious reasons, only a very limited number if any of the older workers are typically part of this pool. Entry into this career phase may move out somewhat as employers begin to take account of increasing working lives, but it is inevitable that employees will keep reaching this stage at some point.

Similarly, in almost any organization, there is a point where the typical employee's salary for valid reasons virtu-ally maxes out. From that point on, raises may be limited, even where performance level remains high. If they are not going to be included in the promotional pool, and they can no longer expect meaningful pay increases, there needs to be other motivators to keep Greyforce engaged in their jobs and careers.

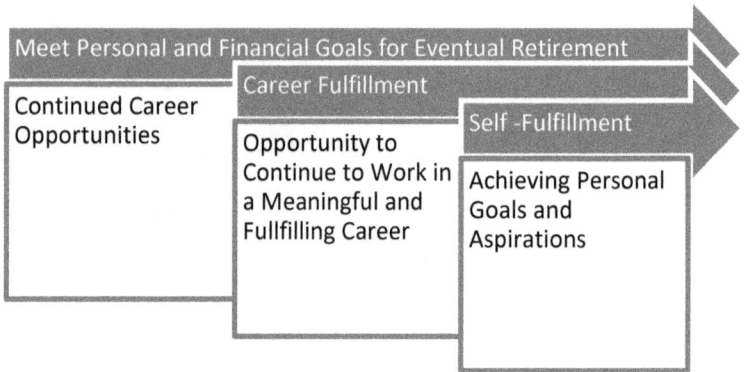

Figure 4. Contributory Career Phase Progression Model

In the contributory phase model in Figure 4, there really isn't a career progression in the traditional sense anymore. The concept of a career "trajectory" is no longer applicable. Parts of this model overlap the others, and they all connect in a different way than the traditional model. Contributory phase workers are not typically motivated by trying to reach the next level in the organization. The progression isn't so much focused on offering a corporate ladder to climb but on offering the opportunity to continue to work productively, having a fulfilling career, and reaching personal goals. This model illustrates what workers typically want from their careers at this stage in their lives. They are likely less interested in promotions or even more money, and more interested in career security and satisfaction. They understand why it is important to both the organization and to themselves that they continue to contribute in a positive way in their careers. They still have energy, skills, ability, and experience to offer their employers, but they must be provided the opportunity to contribute in ways that are different from employees at other stages of their careers.

This model is not intended to preclude the real possibility that many older workers both desire and deserve a chance to continue to advance along the lines of the traditional model but rather to recognize that typically their goals and aspirations of most older workers are likely to be different than their younger counterparts. Indeed, attempting to continue to follow the paradigm applicable to employees at other career stages can become a source of deep frustration and resentment for both employer and employee.

This model shows what the basic needs of many older workers are and how organizations can provide the opportunities for these workers to meet these needs. Organizations that both embrace and publicize this model will be able to support the needs of their older workers as they enter into the contributory phase of their careers. Without an appreciation for the different perspectives of employees at this stage, it is more likely that older workers will continue to experience the fears and frustrations that cause them to disengage and default to limp mode, putting their employers in the unappetizing position of dealing with them as performance problems.

Changing the organization's perceptions about older workers and acknowledging the need to take a critical look at its career progression process could result in more rewarding careers for this growing segment of your workforce while significantly furthering the goals of its business.

Repositioning One's Position

Thinking differently about career progression for Greyforce begins with thinking outside the box when it comes to the definition of a career. The term *career* implies to most employees a progression of positions over a period of time working for one or more organizations. But the concept of career likely takes on a different meaning for members of Greyforce. These individuals are generally less concerned about career progression than they are career security. If they are going to remain fully engaged, members of your Greyforce need to be given a reason to feel secure and confident that their employers have their best interests in mind when it comes to their extended careers. This may take some creative thought and changing certain systems and processes in the organization. Changing the institutional perception that a career trajectory is supposed to be up or out to one that acknowledges and even embraces the concept that a successful career may encompass a final "flat but still dynamic" stage is not necessarily a simple task because it doesn't fit into the traditional model. Everyone needs to understand and support this different approach to career progression.

A Different Kind of Promotion

When you hear the word *promotion* what comes to mind? You likely think of someone getting a more responsible job, more money, greater prestige, progression in the organization's hierarchy, and other perks that may accompany the popular conception of getting promoted. Now think about an older worker desiring to keep working well past his or her normal or expected retirement age in terms of this concept of promotion. Is this model of promotion even realistic for such a worker? Do these unattainable "carrots" actually provide motivation for this group? If not, and the employer is not providing other positive motivators designed for this group, the employer's only alternative form of motivation likely will be the "stick" of negative feedback and explicit or implicit threat of loss of employment.

The fact is that Greyforce workers understand and even accept at some point that they have reached the promotional apex of their careers. Indeed, their values and aspirations are different at this stage of their lives and careers. Instead of gaining ever more responsibility, they may desire less responsibility. Titles may have less meaning or value to them than finding the right role in which they can continue to feel that they are still being successful for the duration or their career.

Finding a New Niche for Greyforce

Your Greyforce employees are a unique segment of your entire employee population that may think and act differently than younger employees. Greyforce doesn't want preferential treatment; they just want to be treated fairly and with respect. They only want to have a chance to be able to contribute by being provided opportunities consistent with their stage in life. The goal should be to keep this group maximally productive by providing enriching work experiences that fit their needs as well as the needs of the organization. The following story illustrates how an employer might do this:

Duty Change

Sylvia Lopez worked for nearly 40 years in the nursing profession, eventually progressing to being in charge of a hospital floor supervising other nurses. The job often was as much counselor to these younger nurses as a boss, giving them advice on their careers as well as on how to balance one's personal and professional lives, something that Sylvia had always done quite well. She had tried to save as much as she could over the years, but as a single parent of two children, she had a difficult time making ends meet. She provided a nice home and was even able to assist her children financially in their college educations, but at the end of the month, there never was much left to prepare for her future retirement needs. This was something that Sylvia just seemed to keep putting off to the future, worrying more about providing for her kids than about her own financial security.

Sylvia had always hoped to retire by the age of 66 when she would qualify for full Social Security and spend more time enjoying her children and grandchildren. But that wasn't in the cards for Sylvia. She found herself at age 66 not having enough money in her hospital-sponsored 401(k) account to be able to comfortably retire after working so hard all her life. Her financial advisor recommended that she continue working full-time as long as possible, at least to age 70. She felt that her only option was to continue working into what she had hoped

---

would be her retirement years. Although her now-grown children offered to have her come live with them to help her financially, that wasn't something that she wanted to do, at least not at this point in her life. Fortunately, her health was still good but the physical strains of being a hospital floor nurse were taking their toll, as were the burdens of working rotating shifts and required overtime. She wondered how she would be able to keep working into her 70s.

Fortunately for Sylvia, she worked for an employer that saw the value of retaining its long-term employees and finding ways to keep them not only employed but fully engaged. Even some of their physicians were experiencing issues similar to Sylvia's as they approached what they had expected to be their retirement ages. They either needed or wanted to work longer, but were also unwilling or unable to keep up the pace the job required. As both physicians and nurses were difficult to replace, the hospital decided it would be in everyone's best interest to create opportunities that better suited the current situations of these long-service employees.

So the hospital decided to afford their older physicians the option of being on-call less often than younger staff members and taking a proportionate reduction in salary. The rigors of taking night and weekend calls had been one of the things that drove doctors into retirement, so reducing their on-call responsibilities was something that was very desirable to this segment of the physician staff. The hospital calculated that this would not cause a backlash among younger doctors because they would perceive this policy as benefiting them too later on in their careers with the hospital.

In Sylvia's case, the hospital offered to create a non-supervisory position with changed duties and more regular hours. Her salary would be less without the overtime she had been working as a charge nurse, but she would still maintain all of her other benefits, including full health care coverage, something especially important to her. This was all a fair and good trade-off as far as she was concerned. As part of her new duties, Sylvia was also asked to establish and coordinate a formal mentoring program for younger nurses, providing instruction and guidance to help them as they progressed in their careers. This was a positive change for Sylvia that met a need of the hospital and at the same time allowed her to continue working as long as she felt she needed to reach her future retirement financial goals.

Fairness Issues

One might ask if there is a fairness issue here by excusing these older workers from responsibilities normally expected to be performed as part of their jobs. As an employer, you might be concerned about setting a precedent by allowing accommodations to be made for your older workers and how others may feel about these actions. This is obviously something that each employer needs to evaluate and decide what is in the best interest of everyone concerned. However, think about these types of adjustments as a sign of your organization's commitment to creating a great working environment for everyone in your workplace, old and young alike. You might be surprised how making what may seem like even a minor exception can make a big difference in how an older employee feels about his or her job. Creating career extending opportunities might make all the difference in getting the most out of older employees who truly desire to continue to be productive contributors in their careers even though they may be working more years than they had planned.

Legal Issues

As we said earlier, any frank discussion of age in the workplace is bound to raise legal concerns that should be reviewed with legal counsel. Age discrimination is unlawful and must be avoided.

However, the approach we are describing is meant to be beneficial to older workers, not detrimental. What we are advocating is a new contributory phase career track, providing alternatives and options to the traditional career track. This model is analogous to the different career tracks offered by law and accounting firms who have had to ditch the "up or out" model because it has caused the premature exit of otherwise terrific employees in whom the firms have a significant investment. They have discovered that many employees wish to avoid the rigors and extreme demands of competing for and then maintaining equity partnership status in favor of a more balanced life style, and they are willing to accept a lower or slower career trajectory in exchange. Many firms now offer a career track designed to provide employees a rewarding career with perhaps less financial upside but also a more balanced life with fewer work demands and more time for themselves and their families.

The fundamental premise, however, is that employees get to elect which track they will be on. If an older worker wishes to remain on the traditional career path, he or she must be allowed to do so and should not be discriminated against or otherwise adversely treated in comparison to their younger peers.

We believe that this approach will lead to fewer bias claims, not more, so long as it is transparent and totally voluntary. The most important thing is that these possibilities be explored and discussions occur between your older workers and their supervisors or managers.

Lessons from the Game of Golf

Many life lessons can be learned from being a golf caddy when you are young. It teaches you a lot about personal behavior and integrity. They say that if you really want to get to know what someone is made up of, play a round of golf with them. Do they count every stroke? Do they play it as it lies, or use the old "foot wedge"? How do they treat their caddy or the locker room attendant? Seeing as a kid how different adults behave on a golf course helps you decide what kind of person you want to become as a grown-up.

Another life lesson from golf is that you can remain competitive even as you age by modifying your game to fit the changes in your physical abilities. Can't hit it as far? Learn to hit it straighter. Need an extra shot to reach the green? Learn to chip and putt better. Want to beat younger, stronger players? Become the embodiment of the old adage, "Drive for show...putt for dough." Your golfing career and your enjoyment of the game do not end just because you have gotten a little older.

The same applies to workers who have entered the contributory phase of their careers. Older employees may no longer be willing or able to keep the same pace they maintained in earlier phases of their careers. But this does not mean that they cannot still be very productive and even competitive. Think about the PGA Senior Golf Tour. Entry into this elite group of professional golfers requires that the players be 50 years of age or older. These players may not be able to boom the ball as far as or be truly competitive with their younger counterparts on the PGA tour, but they can still play marvelously well. And the competitive spirit among members of the Senior Tour is as intense as ever. What a shame it would be if they were relegated to history in their 50s rather than provided a way to extend their careers and showcase their still prodigious talents.

Golf can serve as a model for dealing with the aging of the workforce in your organization. Just like golfers, your senior workers can remain highly productive if offered a senior career path that fits their needs and abilities. They may not be willing or able to perform at the same demanding level they did as younger workers, but they have the wisdom of their experience, which can be a great equalizer. If given the right opportunities, modified to suit their stage in life, they can still make huge contributions to your organization. Is your organization failing to take full advantage of the skills and abilities of its older workforce by expecting them to play under the same conditions as its younger workers when, by simply making a few modifications to suit their stage of life—akin to shortening a few holes—they would still be able to make pars, birdies, and even an occasional hole-in-one for your organization?

Teaching "Old Dogs" New Tricks

Who says you can't teach old dogs new tricks? This type of thinking is one of the most limiting factors when it comes to addressing the needs of Greyforce. Making the decision that an employee is too old to learn something new or that you won't get enough of a return for your training dollars to justify investing in older employees is very problematic. Often we make these assumptions if we believe that our older workers will be retiring in the near or not-too-distant future. This is a mindset that is based on assumptions that are no longer tenable in today's world. It is not only potentially discriminatory, it also risks creating a self-fulfilling prophecy about older workers. You need to ensure that older workers continue to be offered training and development opportunities necessary to enhance their skills and further their careers like everyone else in the organization. Limiting the training opportunities is not only potentially age discrimination and unfair to your older population, it also is an engagement killer for workers who may stay around a lot longer than you think.

Back to the Future Careers

As we said earlier, the up or out career trajectory may not be a suitable model for today's workforce. Maybe we should permit workers the option to go *back to the future*. Just like in the classic movie, an ability to go back in time affords people the ability to change their future. Permitting back to the future career paths can offer this very thing. Many people look back fondly on certain jobs that they may have held at an earlier time in their careers. As they progressed in their careers, they made certain trade-offs or concessions to move to higher, more responsible positions. But what if at their now older age in their careers they would be offered the opportunity to return to this level or position that they really enjoyed in the past? The nature of the work and the responsibility level of these former positions may now be much more conducive to the current needs of these older workers. Placing them into their former roles may be a great move for everyone. This radical notion of permitting voluntarily climbing back down the corporate ladder may be just the right thing to promote career satisfaction for Greyforce employees.

Note, we said "voluntarily." Involuntary demotion is an engagement and morale killer. This is not suggested as a way of dealing with performance problems, but as an option for good employees who are genuinely interested in remaining fully productive, albeit in a lesser role. In order to be effective, a back to the future career option must be formally implemented and defined and clearly something that is available only upon the agreement of both the employee and employer.

One Employer, Two Careers

There is an enlightening icebreaker exercise that is sometimes used to help participants in a training program get to know each other better at the beginning of the session. The facilitator asks each participant what their fantasy career would be if they could be anything they wanted. During this activity, participants express what careers they dream of pursuing if they could currently or eventually when they retire. This exercise typically results in candid insights into each person's real interests and true aspirations in their lives. It is always amazing how divergent many of these participants' dream jobs are from their actual current working careers.

What job do you want next? Is this a question that you would ask someone who is over 65 in your organization (and really mean it)? Probably not unless that person was contemplating what he or she wanted to do after they retire, after already working what used to be considered a career lifetime. This is something that also will likely be changing in the future as older workers continue to remain in the workplace in greater numbers. There is nothing that says that just because someone has 30 or more years in one career profession or discipline that he or she may not be interested in doing something different in their future career, even with the same employer. They may just be ready to go down one of those roads not taken previously and begin a new career journey and adventure.

They used to say that life begins at 40, but that was before. Now they say that 50 is the new 40. We are entering an era when employees are looking for second careers at the age that most employees used to retire. Creating opportunities for second careers that do not require leaving one's current employer can be a very worthwhile endeavor for everyone. There always is something motivating and invigorating about beginning something new in one's career. It can be an exciting prospect for an older employee to make a fresh start in their career much like it was when they first started out in their career. And like anything else new and different, no matter how welcomed and exciting, it can be a bit scary.

Career Counseling for Older Workers

Career counseling is not something that should end on account of age, especially now that retirement at a certain age is no longer a given. Part of your discussions with older workers should include the question of what they would like to do in the future. You might just be amazed at the answers you will hear. Some older workers may want to do something related but different than what they did all their careers. Others may want to try something completely different than the work they have performed for over decades in the past and why not? The possibilities of these career evolutions are endless. Think about the interest and motivation that older workers can bring to their new careers. Talk about getting someone re-engaged in their careers; this may be one of the best ways possible.

Older workers need and want career counseling just like their younger colleagues. Make sure that you provide older workers the same degree of career counseling support and guidance that you would someone just starting out on their new career. Think about what training, resources, experience, and support that an older worker in a new job or career path may need to be successful and provide these resources. If not, you may be setting up these older workers for failure by not providing them the resources they need to be successful.

Retention Strategies for Greyforce Employees

Here is perhaps a novel thought: What if you began thinking about ways to keep older workers working longer and better rather than trying to figure out ways to off-board them from the organization as they get older. This would indicate that you understand and greatly value the potential contributions that older workers can still provide for the organization. What would you do differently if you had this mindset about your older workers? You would want to find out what they needed to keep them happy and productive in their jobs and ensure that you provided these things. You might even end up recruiting Greyforce workers as you search for outside talent to bring into your organization. There may be some real bargains to be had out there, if you are open to them.

Benefits Redesign

Benefits packages are designed to further the company's business by assisting in the retention, recruitment, and continuing engagement of workers. However, if you look at the current overall benefits package offered to employees, you may find that they are designed for a specific segment of your organization. Probably these benefits were designed for employees raising families, and this is fine for those individuals. But what about your older workers' benefits package? At this point in their lives, they are not concerned about benefits packages offering such things as dependent care, orthodontist coverage, or well-baby examinations. What about offering these employees benefits specifically designed for their needs?

If you accept that your workforce will include an increasing proportion of older workers, why would you not want your benefits package to assist you in keeping these employees satisfied and fully engaged? You most likely will find that your current benefits program does not adequately address the needs of your older workers. There may be a need to revamp the coverages as well as design of the benefits packages you offer your Greyforce employees. This could include more flexible benefits packages that continue to change to address the different needs of older employees as they age.

The Advantage of Being an Older Worker

Yes, there are advantages to being a member of Greyforce. For one thing, they may be past worrying about many of the things they worried about when they were younger as their values and ambitions have changed. They are likely less concerned about prestige and more concerned about job fulfillment and satisfaction. They probably do not worry as much as their younger peers about the size of their offices or if their boss is paying enough attention to them.

Older workers may be more comfortable speaking up for those issues about which they feel strongly as they have learned that those on top do not always know all the answers. They have already proven themselves and know what they are capable of achieving. They just want to be provided the opportunity to continue to contribute. They are comfortable in their own skins and less focused on trying to be someone or something they are not. And they may no longer take the opportunity to continue to keep working for granted as they may have when they were younger. These are all desirable characteristics to be found in an employee of any age.

As illustrated earlier, all assumptions about when employees will leave the workforce for retirement need to be thrown out the window. The assumption, unless told otherwise, should be that Greyforce employees are in it for the long haul. In many ways, we need to change our mindset about employees working into what we used to think as their old age. The term *old age* is even becoming a misnomer as we understand that aging is increasingly an individualized process, affecting different people differently. For most types of jobs, a particular age can no longer be presumed to be associated with loss of ability to perform a job.

In fact, as they age, many employees may become more astute at capitalizing on the natural abilities that helped them become successful during their younger years. They may even be able to reshape themselves to make their age and experience into an asset rather than a detriment, much like aging screen idols may do by embracing parts that celebrate their maturity, wisdom, and continued mental and physical vitality rather than pathetically attempting to create the illusion that they are ageless. Older people know who they are. They have already had what used to be considered a "lifetime of experience" in the workplace and are poised to utilize their abilities and attributes to continue to be successful in the later stages of their careers.

As pointed out previously, older workers may have differing goals and aspirations. Some will be looking for a way to continue working that acknowledges that they are no longer on an ascending career trajectory but still affords them an opportunity to meaningfully contribute. Others may want to continue to compete for higher positions. The fact that they are still willing and able to contribute at a high level despite reaching what used to be retirement age gives them an expanded timeline for achieving their career goals, and there should be no reason for arbitrarily taking them off the future promotion lists just because of their age. Indeed, the fact that employees will be working longer can potentially change the ultimate career achievements of the Greyforce generation. They now have more time to achieve their career aspirations and goals. They may have also gained greater patience waiting for these aspirations to be fulfilled. They only need their employers to recognize that they are still in the game and give them a fair chance to compete for a starting position.

Work/Life Balance: It's Not Just a Young Worker's Issue

When you hear the discussion about work/life balance, we often associate this with the needs of young parents trying to deal with the pressures of work and raising a young family. Many organizations have developed initiatives including work-at-home programs that allow parents of young children to avoid the high cost of daycare as well as be present in the home during their children's developmental years.

But what about this work/life balance for older workers? This same concept could also be a benefit to this segment of your employee population as well. There might be certain health or medical needs of older workers that could best be accommodated in their own homes specially adapted to their needs. And this group has its own family obligations that would make the ability to work at home a much appreciated option—the reality is that Boomers are now often primary care givers to their aged parents.

Modified work schedules could be another change that could help enable older workers to remain employed longer such was the case in the story about Sylvia Lopez. Older workers may have difficulty putting in the hours necessary to keep up with the increasingly faster pace of business today. Changing or modifying these schedules or workday expectations could also be a big help for older workers.

Retirement could also be turned into a planned phasing-out process rather than a hard stop as has traditionally been the case. Older workers could begin reducing their working hours (and compensation) over time while focusing on those aspects of their jobs most important and critical to the organization, including the process of deciding what will be done with their work when they are gone. In this phased approach, everyone gains. Employees are able to continue working while spending more time tending to the needs of themselves and their families and gradually transitioning into this major life changing status. The organization continues to benefit from the employee's skills, knowledge, and abilities while it has the time to plan for the intending retiree's departure in a more orderly fashion.

Chapter 4: Discussion Points

This chapter introduces the term *grayforce* to describe the growing presence of older workers in the workplace today.

> ➢ What do you envision the impact of greyforce to be in your organization?

> ➢ What are the potential benefits of having these experiences and talented people remaining employed in their careers?

> ➢ What are some of the challenges of keeping your greyforce employees engaged in their careers?

The chapter also discusses the concept of a collaborative employment agreement between employers and members of their greyforce workforce to help them remain working longer in their careers.

> ➢ What would this look like in your organization?

Think about the mindset described in this chapter concerning unconscious age bias and older employees "not having enough runway" to be considered for future promotions.

> ➢ Do these mindsets exist in your organization?

> ➢ If so, what potential problems does this mindset present?

> ➢ How can this be changed in your organization?

What is your view on the value of experience concerning greyforce employees?

> ➢ Do you agree that it can be perceived as a double-edged sword as described in this chapter?

> ➢ Do you agree that the past is prolog to the future and that greyforce can potentially help you see this if given the opportunity? What are some examples?

> ➤ Do you believe that change actually comes in cycles if you step back far enough to see the similarities and patterns? Why or why not? What are some examples?

> ➤ Do you agree that your greyforce employees can help you see these cycles and help you better prepare for their arrivals? How?

In reviewing the Traditional Career Progression Model and the Greyforce Career Progression models, what is the greatest distinction between the two in your opinion?

> ➤ How can you create career opportunities for greyforce employees consistent with their career progression model in your organization that would benefit both these older employees and your organization?

How do you feel about the potential "fairness" issues concerning making certain job changes for greyforce employees?

> ➤ How would you deal with these issues should they arise?

Do you feel that it would make good business sense for your organization to actually try to retain and actually recruit greyforce employees? Why or why not?

If you are a golfer or just a fan, what do you envision could be your older worker's best "short game" that can, in actuality, produce the most productive results?

Chapter 5

Generational Diversity as a Strategy for Success

Most organizations do not usually think about ensuring that they have a certain level of generational diversity in their organizational structure or on their teams, but rather rely on this happening on its own. They accept generational diversity as a fact of life but do not see any inherent usefulness to it. They thus fail to recognize the value that strategic use of generational diversity can bring to their organizations. Think about the value that older employees bring to virtually any organizational structure or team when their experience and wisdom are brought to bear on any decision-making process in your organization. And think about what younger workers learn from these older experienced employees. Think about the synergies that could be attained by strategically combining the inputs of older and younger workers.

With so much focus on the novel challenge of dealing with the millennial generation entering the workforce today, it is easy to overlook the value of the older generation. Most organizations are concerned about retaining their younger talented workers who are considered the future of the company. They spend all kinds of resources recruiting, training, and nurturing these workers, often only to see them lured away for a few more dollars by the competition. Perhaps in such situations the employers have neglected the importance to retention of making the case that a fulfilling career depends on more than dollars and cents. Young workers may tend to focus impatiently on the here and now, but they are not totally heedless of the intangibles that make one company a better place to work than another. Part of making your organization a more desirable place to remain employed is providing an enriched work environment in which workers of all ages are provided opportunities to reach their career aspirations. If your senior workers give off a vibe of excitement, fulfillment, and engagement, it may just help you to attract and retain those younger workers as well.

Think about what can be gained by ensuring and leveraging generational diversity throughout your organization. Most organizations simply assume that knowledge will be passed down, but there is no plan for making sure this happens in the most effective ways. By being strategic about use of your most experienced workers, you can ensure that your millennials benefit from their wisdom and experiences. You can offer your younger generation of employees an MBA's worth of case studies in business taught by those who have experienced these cases first hand. What could be better than that?

Older workers too can benefit from the energy, ideas, and technical knowledge of their younger counterparts. Think about how consciously and creatively combining the knowledge of both generations could result in synergies not before realizable in previous generations. Consider how linking younger and older generations in mutually supportive mentoring relationships could accelerate this synergy and growth potential for both generations.

High-Tech Lesson on the Strategic Use of Generational Diversity

The following is a story about how traditional business concepts can be applied to a high technology business venture to achieve better overall results.

CompWare Systems started as the brainchild of Richard Smethport, a wealthy entrepreneur who wanted to expand his business portfolio into high technology. His family had made their fortune in the oil field business a century ago and it was still amassing big profits as a result of the oil and natural gas resurgence of recent years. Richard had been looking for ways to diversify his investment portfolio, having learned the importance of diversification from his grandfather, who had observed the fortunes of others rise and fall with the price of natural energy over his lifetime.

As a young boy, he would listen to his grandfather tell him stories of his early days working in the oil fields in Pennsylvania at the time when the fossil fuels industry was on the verge of booming as a result of the nation's new love affair with the automobile. But the boom seemed to be short lived, at least in terms of fortunes to be made in the oil fields of Pennsylvania in the early part of the 1900s.

As the easily available rich crude oil was relatively quickly pumped out of the ground using the best technology of the time, the oil boom towns seemed to quickly disappear along with the fortunes of many early investors. Fortunately for Richard, his grandfather had greater insight. He diversified the family fortunes into other related energy investments, making good decisions that still to this day continued to pay dividends. One of the wise decisions his grandfather made was to retain the mineral rights in the extensive land holdings of the family throughout Northwestern Pennsylvania. He believed that they had only tapped a small portion of the oil laying beneath the surface in these once rich oil fields and dreamed of the day when what he called "second recovery" could be possible to extract the remainder of the oil from these fields.

What Richard's grandfather couldn't have envisioned was just how long it would actually take for his dream to come to fruition. It was nearly a century before oil field technology would rejuvenate this industry to anything near its early days, and Richard was certainly the benefactor of his grandfather's vision. The riches from these previously untapped assets were flowing into the family's coffers and the job of preserving them was Richard's. He looked for an opportunity to diversify his family's assets but wanted to find an industry as exciting as the oil business was in his grandfather's day. The software industry seemed to fit the bill.

Richard had become a wise investor and businessman in his own right. He had gone to one of the top business schools in the country and graduated with honors. He never seemed to take the easy route despite his family fortune. He had chosen to work for several high tech companies as a young man to gain experience in this business before attempting to start up his own company. By the time he was ready to start CompWare Systems, he had become a wise businessman, very much like his great grandfather. Richard had learned that becoming a successful leader is all about making good decisions. Following in his grandfather's footsteps, Richard did not act hastily when it came to making important business decisions. Richard realized that being successful in business was really all about having the right people involved in helping you make these decisions. He had also come to recognize that just building up your executive team with a bunch of young stereotypic graduate business school clones affirming your every decision may not be the best idea. He realized that having a diversity of perspectives around the table could result in better decisions, ones like his great grandfather had made, ones that would yield positive results for years, even generations, to come.

By the time that Richard was ready to start up CompWare Systems, he was in his 40s, practically a ripe old age by industry standards. He was very familiar with all of the perceptions about today's millennials, especially in the computer software industry having spent the past several decades in this business. As he built his leadership team for the new company, he intentionally avoided loading it up with only technological Wunderkinder as did many others in the industry. Richard understood the importance of having a balance of generational diversity even in a fast-paced, quickly changing industry that seems to reinvent itself every nanosecond. Richard understood that there were certain principles of business and success that transcended time and fashion. To the surprise and even concern of others, more than half of the leadership team Richard brought into the new company were in their 50s or older. There were those who began predicting that Richard's new company would quickly get left behind in this dynamic and ultracompetitive business by their youth-oriented competitors.

Richard had learned that a person's leadership style and capabilities to a certain extent were related to age. He believed that leadership style often evolves and matures as people get older and that that you didn't have to be a behavioral expert to be a good judge of people.

Richard was astute enough to perceive that every generation had its differences and strengths. He thought a great deal about his grandfather's generation and the times in which he was raised. This was a generation that had no sense of entitlement. They believed that you had to work for everything you got in life, and they were willing to make just about any sacrifice to find their way in this world. They respected authority and were more inclined to do what they were told without complaint or challenge and be loyal to their employer until the day they stopped working not expecting any additional support from their former employer.

Richard perceived his generation, the Baby Boomers, as being highly driven toward personal success. They too were willing to sacrifice to be successful but wanted to have more control over their lives and careers than did their parents and grandparents. Boomers are not a silent generation. They felt they should have a voice in things and did not believe in blindly kowtowing to the judgment of their elders. They were more likely than prior generations to question authority in the workplace if they disagreed. They wanted to learn and valued educational achievement and preparation. Boomers paid lip service to the value of work/life balance but were not very successful in achieving it. They were willing to work even harder than their parents had worked in order to obtain the trappings of material success at an earlier age. Boomers were less loyal to their employers than their parents and would always be looking for that bigger better deal.

Richard had worked with many of the so-called millennials during his career and began to gain insight into this younger generation in the workplace. They were willing to work hard to get ahead but when they talked about wanting work/life balance, they meant it. They were raised on technology and were much more comfortable with technology than any previous generations. Richard noticed that this group was much less impressed with titles and more focused on knowledge and ability, although they do respect authority. They had been taught in school to work and interact in teams more than their older counterparts. Richard noticed that they wanted recognition and praise more often and would react negatively if it was not provided when they felt it was deserved. This group had far less loyalty to their employer than any previous generations, due at least in part to their perception, an accurate perception, that today's employers have less loyalty to their employees than ever before. They neither expected, nor really wanted to spend their careers working for just one or two employers.

These were interesting generational differences to Richard, and he gave a great deal of thought about how best to make use of them on his leadership team. He wanted to avoid the currently popular stereotypic employment model of hiring only the brightest young graduates from the best technology programs in the country. And he did not want to create a college campus type atmosphere fostered by some high tech companies that he believed would be more of a unsustainable distraction than a benefit. Richard did appreciate the need to break down many of typical organizational bureaucracies that could have a limiting effect on creativity and teamwork in an organization, but he also respected many of the traditional work structures of the past that valued age and experience. He didn't want his new company to become just a "think tank," working on interesting ideas and new experimental design without a clear blueprint for success.

His vision was to balance the best of the new organizational structures with time-proven organizational designs. The key, he believed, was in using generational diversity to make his start-up company successful. He wanted his company to have both talented younger people who could bring innovative ideas to the table and experienced leaders with the knowledge and expertise to successfully bring these ideas successfully to market.

Chapter 5: Discussion Points

Does your organization give consideration to the generational diversity of your organizational structure or teams as they are established, or does the existence of any such diversification just happen by chance?

> ➢ What do you see as the potential advantages to ensuring that you have the optimum generational diversity balance in all of the functions of your organization in the future?

> ➢ How do you think that the different generations in your organization could benefit and learn from one another if you ensured that you have this balance in your organization?

This chapter discusses the concept of the distribution of age in certain functions of an organization, citing the example of the average age of a typical board of directors of an organization. As expected, the average age of this group is likely to be higher than other functions in an organization.

> ➢ Why do you think this would be the case?

> ➢ How could the concept of age distribution be extended to other functions in your organization?

> ➢ What potential does this concept have for your grey-force employees to make a greater contribution?

In the story presented in this chapter about when Richard Smethport was starting up his software company, what do you believe were the most important lessons, especially concerning generational diversity, that he learned from his grandfather's experience as a century ago in the oil fields of Pennsylvania?

> ➢ Do you agree with Richard's assessment of the generational differences in today's workplace?

➢ How do they differ from your own experiences?

➢ Do you believe that Richard created the right balance of generational diversity in his new organization or were his critics right that he wasn't bringing in enough young tech-savvy talent? Why or why not?

➢ Do you believe that CompWare Systems will be successful based on what you learned in this story? Why or why not?

Chapter 6

Creative Use of Your Greyforce Employees

We have suggested that employers should begin taking a different approach to managing the careers of their Greyforce workers, one that embraces the actual wants, needs, and abilities of workers whose careers are now being extended because of the new realities of aging, health, and economics. We have called this final stage of employment the contributory phase because workers in it are still willing and able to contribute to the organization and can be fully engaged even after they have realized that they are at or even beyond the apex of their careers. In this chapter, we will make a few suggestions of ways employees in this phase may continue to achieve job fulfillment while making meaningful contributions beyond merely working out their time.

Filling the Gaps

What gaps do you now have that could be filled by the older segment of your employee population? Which projects would you love to have completed but just don't have the manpower to complete? Those projects just might be perfect for an older worker who would prefer to focus on one task exclusively and not be burdened by the other responsibilities of his current job.

Knowledge Transfer

If you are like many organizations concerned that the knowledge will disappear when these older workers do eventually retire, you might consider various ways in which older workers may become engaged in transferring their knowledge for the benefit of the organization.

One way to do this is by creating a mentoring program in which older workers spend time with younger workers with the purpose of making certain that their knowledge, expertise, and wisdom are passed on to the next generation. Being asked to act as a mentor is different from simply being asked to train one's eventual replacement. Mentorship can be very gratifying to the employees involved. For the older workers, being asked to mentor provides a feeling of affirmation and respect. It is energizing to be given a new assignment. For the younger worker, a mentor is a resource that can guide them in making sure that they are doing the right things and getting the right tools to assure them future success in their careers.

Another way of involving older workers in the transfer of their expertise would be enlisting them in building a database as a repository for their knowledge that could be accessed by future workers. Creation of such a database would engage older workers in a very positive way in helping to ensure the future success of the organization. Your older workers are really a valuable resource. It is a shame to think how much is lost by failing to recognize and exploit their value by just letting them wither on the vine in the final years of their careers.

Greyforce Special Corps

Whether you know it or not, the rest of the world already appreciates the value of your older workers. There is an organization, the Service Corps of Retired Executives (SCORE), devoted to connecting retired executives with businesses in need of their expertise on a volunteer basis. Think about the possibility of having a special services function in your organization, providing career opportunities for your older workers different than the traditional jobs that are part of your organization's normal organizational structures. This special services function could help the organization solve the most difficult problems of the day or bring ideas to be more competitive in the future. Imagine the results that could be achieved by unleashing the expertise and creativity of this group. The combined knowledge, experience, and expertise your Greyforce brings to the table is a resource you should be tapping into.

Redefining Normal Responsibilities

In addition to new work opportunities, consider how your organizational systems need to adapt to these new workforce demographics. Many of the traditional aspects of employment may need to change to support these older workers, such as work schedules, physical work locations, benefits programs, reporting relationships, job designs, and incentive compensation programs. For instance, does employment necessarily mean reporting every week to work for 40 hours or could it be some other schedule? Do not let yourself become confined by your traditional perceptions and rules for what is expected as "normal" employment procedures and processes. How could you redefine responsibilities for this segment of your organization that could better meet their needs?

Here is a story of a valuable employee who wanted and needed to continue working past age 65 but struggled with the existing work requirements of his position. This story shows how his employer was able to find a way to both meet his needs and still be able to benefit from his years of experience:

Office at the Beach

Roger Wilson had a very successful career as a stock broker for one of the largest investment firms in the country. Earlier in his career, he had managed both a major metropolitan office and eventually was responsible for multiple offices in the northeast region of the country. Later on in his career, he had successfully managed the investment portfolios for some of the wealthiest families in America. Roger enjoyed his job but also looked forward to retiring someday enjoying the financial success he had earned over the years. But even talented investment experts sometimes find themselves in financial straits. Roger and his family loved the ocean and had invested much of their assets in beach property in the southeast coastal areas of the United States, expecting prices to continue to escalate as they had in the past decades.

But an economic recession had hit these real estate markets hard. Property values suddenly plummeted to levels well below their previous peak value. Unfortunately, Roger had invested heavily in a number of speculative beach properties almost at the height of the market and now found himself in personal financial difficulty for the first time in his life. Roger began to think that his dreams of an early and financially comfortable retirement may be fading away. Roger now found himself at what he expected to be his retirement age, having financial problems that required him to keep working but fearing that he would be physically unable to put in the hours he used to in his younger years to get this situation corrected. In fact, Roger was concerned that he would no longer be able to adequately perform the job that he had been so successful in.

Roger's boss and long-time colleague came up with the solution. He suggested that Roger move from their New York headquarters to the beach where he already had a vacation home and work from there full time. His boss suggested that Roger make his own hours of work and not be confined to normal business day hours or even a traditional Monday through Friday workweek. In fact, many of Roger's biggest clients were also retired and living near the area where he would relocate to. They would not mind if he met with them during nontraditional days or hours of the week, in fact they preferred meeting at these times. This arrangement suited Roger's personal needs and, better yet, provided a unique service to the company's clients.

Sometimes breaking away from the conventional ways of structuring a job is the key to keeping older workers both productive and happy in their extended careers. Identifying these ways to accommodate older workers should be part of the business strategy of every organization. Again, this requires a different perception and acceptance of the continuing value of older workers. Instead of ignoring this segment of your workforce because they will be leaving soon, you need to be thinking of ways to continue to maximize their contributions to the organization. Just like in Roger's case, you will probably need to develop a "new normal" in order to get the best out of and retain your oldest generation of employees. Breaking some of the rules may be necessary and wholly appropriate.

The lesson here is that in today's workplace, if you want to keep your workforce engaged, the old paradigm of treating everybody the same may have to give way to a paradigm based on assessment of individuals' needs and wants at the various stages of their careers.

Chapter 6: Discussion Points

Do you agree that 80 could become the new 60 in terms of age in the workplace of the future?

> ➤ If not 80, what do you think will be the future equivalent of age 60 in the workplace?

Think about some of the job design changes described in this chapter to help older workers be more comfortable in their work environments.

> ➤ What impact do you think that these changes could have on these employees' ability to continue working longer in their careers?

> ➤ Does your organization have any programs that focus specifically on helping older employees continue working longer in their careers? If not, what might be some benefits of establishing such programs?

> ➤ Do you believe that older workers may be reluctant to ask for help on their own? Why?

> > – What could you do to make older workers feel more comfortable requesting help?

What are your feelings about providing older workers with different performance standards and evaluation systems than their younger counterparts?

> ➤ Could this create "fairness" issues for the younger generation in your workplace?

> ➤ How would you address these issues should they present themselves in your organization in the future?

In reading the story about stockbroker Roger Wilson, how did breaking some of the work rules concerning where and when he could perform his job make such a big difference?

➤ What do you think might have happened instead if the stock brokerage firm did not help Roger by allowing him to work from his home at the beach?

➤ Does your organization sometimes get too focused on following every company policy and procedure to the detriment of your older workers' needs? If so, how can this change?

Chapter 7

Helping Employees Age Gracefully in Their Careers

Advancing age is ultimately the great equalizer: it inevitably affects everyone. Thinking about how to help older workers be successful is in everyone's best interest. Managers and supervisors need to understand and relate to their older employees. Those who have not yet joined Greyforce need to think about how they will want to be treated in the final phases of their careers.

What older workers really want as they continue to extend their careers is to be treated with dignity and respect while being given the opportunity to contribute to their organization's success. Helping employees age gracefully in their careers should be the goal of every employer. Think about how you can help older employees continue to contribute and feel the same sense of accomplishment that they did earlier in their careers even though they realize that their careers and earning potential may have maxed out. Greyforce employees need to feel that they are leading a productive and fulfilled life during this extended stage of their careers.

Delayed retirement does not mean one must miss all of the pleasures of retirement. First, employees generally can expect to live and remain healthy and active longer, so there will still be time for a real retirement. Second, as we have suggested, creative career design can give older workers more freedom to strike a different balance between work and personal life, one geared to allowing the employee to take the foot off the pedal a bit at work and throttle up on outside pursuits. The key is having all parties recognize the benefits to be had for everyone and then buy in to the changes that are necessary to achieve this.

Becoming the CEO of One's Career and Retirement

If they are going to continue to remain positive and be fully engaged while working, Greyforce employees need to feel that they are in control of how and when they will eventually retire. They need to be the CEO of their careers and future retirement plans. It is important that they feel empowered by their employer in this endeavor. They would like to have not only the support of their organizations but also choices and viable options when it comes to working longer. They prefer to be able to determine when and how their careers will eventually end without feeling pressured to exit before they are ready. Believe it or not, they would like a dialogue with you about, and a game plan for, their transition into retirement—one that goes beyond the traditional planning for managing their finances and benefits after retirement, but also includes managing the remainder of their careers before retirement.

Chapter 7: Discussion Points

Do you agree that age is ultimately the greater equalizer, eventually affecting everyone indiscriminately?

- ➢ What do you think this means to your organization?
- ➢ What does this mean to you personally concerning your career and retirement planning?

If you are not yet old enough to be a member of Greyforce, think about how you will want to be treated when you reach this stage in your career.

- ➢ What do you think will be most important to you at that time?
- ➢ How will that be different than what is most important today to you concerning your career?

Do you agree that delayed retirement does not mean that one can't enjoy his or her later years in life?

- ➢ What do you think this means to your Greyforce employees?
- ➢ If you find yourself in this situation, what would this mean to you?

Think about the statement, "You need to become the CEO of your future retirement plans."

- ➢ What do you think this means to your Greyforce employees?
- ➢ What does this mean to you and your future retirement plans?

Summary

There is a new reality today when it comes to career longevity: working lives will be longer. The goal for all organizations should be finding ways to keep all their employees—whether brand new or very seasoned—fully engaged at each and every phase of their extended careers.

Your organization needs to seek ways for your Greyforce to succeed rather than secede prematurely (either physically or mentally) from your organization. You need to find a way to permit these employees to continue contributing rather than becoming problems that need to be dealt with. We need a new compact, governing the work relation based on a creative rethinking and perhaps reconfiguration of the expectations and requirements of the employment relationship for older employees.

Engaging older workers can provide many benefits for everyone. The challenge will be to find new ways to tap in to and leverage the talent and abilities of employees as they work longer.

Finding oneself or one's employees in the position of needing or wanting to work beyond what once was considered normal retirement age should not feel like being dealt a bad hand. The ability to keep working longer should be considered a blessing. Delaying retirement is not a failure in one's career. It can provide a great opportunity for everyone in the organization, young and old alike.

Age really is all about perspective!

Appendix

Engaging Older Workers Organizational Assessment

1. Have you studied the changing age demographics in your organization? If so, do you see a change in the average retirement age of your employees?

   Suggestions:

   - Develop a study of the average retirement age of your employees over the past 5 to 10 years to see if there is a change or trend in this data.

   - Review this data with your employees to help open a dialog on this subject and solicit their ideas and suggestions on how to address any changes or trends revealed by these studies.

2. Do you have any programs currently or planned in your organization that address the needs of this growing segment of your employee population??

   Suggestions:

   - As a result of the dialog suggested above, develop various task forces to further study and analyze any significant changes in these older employee demographics.
   - Based on this data, present recommendations to the senior leadership of your organization concerning these changes and trends.

3. Have you developed programs or processes to help your managers and supervisors comfortably discuss the needs of their older employees, especially those who decide to continue working beyond their normal retirement age?

    Suggestions:

    -   Develop training programs or counseling sessions for your supervisors and managers to help them better understand how to comfortably and legally discuss the needs of their older employees.

    -   Listen to the feedback and suggestions of this group concerning how to best enable older workers to continue to work beyond their normal retirement age productively and in a satisfying manner possible for everyone.

4. Do your older workers feel that they can express their concerns about working longer in their careers and that their voice will be heard?

    Suggestions:

    -   Develop forums for older workers to express their concerns, needs, as well as career goals.

    -   Ensure that managers and supervisors communicate the concerns of their older workers to their supervisors and that action is taken on this feedback as appropriate.

5. Has your organization thought about the potential contributions that older workers can make and how to support their potential?

    Suggestions:

    *   Act upon the suggestions you hear both from older workers and their supervisors concerning how to support older workers and help them make their greatest contributions to your organization.

    *   Think outside the box when it comes to tapping in to the potential of your older workforce even if it is not consistent with certain current policies and practices of the organization.

6. Have you considered how the culture of your organization will be changed by the growing emergence of Greyforce in your employee population and are you prepared for this change?

    Suggestions:

    *   Think about your organization's culture and who it is most focused on concerning promotional and developmental opportunities. Most likely you will find that it is focused mostly on younger employees or those in the middle of their careers.

    *   Consider how you can change this younger centric culture to also include your older Greyforce employees for these same opportunities.

7. Are your current employee benefits programs adequate to address the needs of your Greyforce employees?

Suggestions:

- Review your current employee benefits programs to see what segment of your employee population they are most focused on serving. Again, you likely will find that they are designed to serve your younger rather than older active employees.

- Talk to your older employees remaining in the workplace beyond their normal retirement age about what benefits are most important to them and design these changes into your benefits programs.

8. Have you developed programs to "capture" the experience and knowledge of your Greyforce employees for the benefit of future generations of workers?

Suggestions:

- Begin the process of finding ways to capture the knowledge and experience of your older employees before they are about to leave the organization.

- Think of creative ways to use the new technologies available to enable this knowledge to be captured for the use of future generations of employees.

9. Have you considered how Greyforce employees fit into your current career development processes and what changes in these processes may be necessary in the future?

Suggestions:

- Ensure that your older employees are discussed during any management development reviews or discussions in your organization.

- Train managers and supervisors to ensure that all qualified older workers should be part of the pool of potential candidates for any promotional opportunities in your organization.

10. Do your current recognition programs adequately and fairly include the older employees in your organization?

Suggestions:

- Review your current recognition programs to see if younger employees receive a disproportionate amount of recognition to the exclusion of older employees.

- Develop special recognition programs for older employees to acknowledge their contributions and value to the organization.

www.ingramcontent.com/pod-product-compliance
Lightning Source LLC
Chambersburg PA
CBHW071213200326
41519CB00018B/5499